THE MENTAL PLAYBOOK

An Ultimate Blueprint on How to Become a High Achiever

By Making Your Mind Your GREATEST Asset

By Eugene Johnson

MOTIVATING
THE MASSES

Published by Motivating the Masses
http://motivatingthemasses.com/

The Mental Playbook may be purchased for educational, business, or sales promotional use. For more information, please email the special marketing department at TheMentalPlaybook@zyrl.us

An extension of the copyright page appears in the back of the book.

FIRST EDITION

Book cover designed by Myrna Urmanita
Library of Congress Cataloging-in-Publication Data has been applied for.

DEDICATION

I want to first and foremost thank my Lord and Savior,
Jesus Christ, for without God's grace, I wouldn't even
be alive to write this book!

This book is also dedicated to my amazing wife, Josephine,
and son, Nathaniel, without whom I would not be
who I am today. From the bottom of my heart, I
would like to say thank you
for putting up with my craziness and loving me
through this journey. You guys are the air I breathe
and the heartbeat in my chest.
I love you both so much!

This book is also dedicated to my mother, Joanne.
You have been an inspiration to me. Every time I
wanted to quit,
I thought about what you had to go through, and I
persevere.
Thank you for loving me though my ups and downs,
and fighting the fight only single moms truly understand.
I love you!

Table of Contents

INTRODUCTION

In today's generation,
most people know more about the operating power
in a smartphone than the
operating power in their own head.

Every time I read a book, watch a training video, or go to a seminar about mindset, I find myself saying, "I get it, but I am confused. How do I apply this to my life again?" The idea of mindset shouldn't be this difficult thing to digest and understand. The problem is that when most people talk about the topic of the seminar, they go in one of two ways.

The first way is, the trainer will be so scientific that they lose us in all of the neuroscience jargon and psychotherapy lingo. They use words and terms like *association cortex*, *neurotransmitter*, *cerebrum*, *parietal lobe*, *homeostasis*, and *signal transduction pathways*. The average person has no clue (half of the time, I don't either) about what those terms really mean and how to use that information to tap into higher levels of their mental capacity.

The second way the trainers will lose us is by going all metaphysical and weird, and start talking about priming, transmittal energy, and vibrations. Though all of these things have merit, when the average person who has never encountered this type of training before hears that they "need to sit for 20 minutes on the ground, Indian style, talking to themselves and channeling the vibrations into their life," it sounds a bit crazy. I know it sounded crazy to me. When I first heard it, I took the famous words of Michael Blackson in the first *Friday* movie: "I can't get jiggy with this …"

The problem with these two styles of teaching the topic of mindset is that they don't allow me to take the information and turn it into something practical that I can use in my everyday life. We all know that the brain is powerful; we all know that we have not scratched the surface of understanding what the brain can do; and we all know that if we could tap into more of its power, then we could achieve some amazing things.

WE
ALL
KNOW
THAT WE
HAVE
NOT
SCRACHED
THE SURFACE OF
UNDERSTANDING
WHAT THE
BRAIN CAN DO

#TheMentalPlaybook
#MentalAsset

Now, as I say that, you might be thinking about the movie *Limitless* with Bradley Cooper, but I promise that you do not need to take some "special pill" to tap into more of your mental power. You also don't need to become a professor in neuroscience to understand the functions of the brain and how to use it to achieve what you want. All you need is some simple and practical understanding of basic mental functions to create any success you want, and at any time!

Keep in mind that I am not saying all of the technical understandings of the brain and its functions are irrelevant in the grand scheme of life. What I am saying is that the average person, one who didn't go to an Ivy League school to understand the concepts in a technical way, would be able to understand them when they are broken down in a way that makes sense in everyday life. That is something the average person can get behind. Everyone may not know how to operate a rocket ship, but we can operate our smartphones.

Imagine that your brain is like your smartphone, but instead of using your smartphone to do all the amazing things it can do—like download apps, browse the internet, take pictures, play games, check your social pages, etc.—you only use it to make calls. Is it okay to just use a smartphone to make calls? Of course it is, but why waste the power of its other functionalities? In today's generation, most people know more about the operating power in a smartphone than the operating power in their own head. Today, most people are using their brains for basic calling. They use it to think at work, to drive a car, and to cook, but it can also build rocket ships, solve the most complicated math equations, and create massive business empires. Because the average person doesn't know how to use their brain to do some of the more complex stuff, they settle for the average stuff and consider the people who have decided to use their brains for those other things either geniuses or lucky. My mentor used to tell me that luck is just "Labor Under Correct Knowledge."

The reason I called this book *The Mental Playbook* was because I am a big sports fan and a former athlete, and I know that coaches design playbooks to win championships. If a team is together on the same page with the right playbook, the right players, and the right desire, they can and should win the championship. I believe that the principles in this book are the very plays that you need to and should run in order to win the championship in your life. I give you this playbook not just to read but to study the plays and work on becoming better every single day. If you do that, I will be talking about you and how you went from ordinary to extraordinary, how you went from average to high achiever.

This book will be broken up into two sections. In the first section, I will present to you a framework that I have been studying and using since I was a teenager, which I call the Mental Matrix. This is the place I believe any mindset training should begin. In the second section of the book, I will present to you the achievement playbook—the 10 key ways of thinking that separate the average from the high achiever and some practical strategies and stories that you can learn from immediately and apply in your life.

For the past several years, I have been studying, practicing, and teaching these tactics to myself as well as sales leaders, corporate executives, entrepreneurs,

Luck IS JUST LABOR UNDER CORRECT KNOWLEDGE

#TheMentalPlaybook
#MentalAsset

and other leaders of industries. Before knowing any of this, I was a lost kid looking for direction. I knew I had more to give to life, and I wanted to understand how. Through these principles, I have been able to gain better relationships, grow myself personally and professionally, and have a healthier and happier life. I have been able to take these strategies and change my net worth from starting with a negative sign to now starting with an *M*!

These were things I could only dream about as a kid growing up, but we can all take those dreams we have out of our heads and make them a reality. This book is about just that. In this book, I will tell a lot of the backstories of my life, some of which I have never told out loud before, but these stories will tell about the journey I have been on and the mental lessons I learned along the way. Believe me, this life is a journey, and I have not yet arrived, but I have learned some things that I believe might be able to assist you as you go on your journey to your promised land. I've also been inspired by many friends, mentors, and family members who have helped me throughout my journey, and I hope to take some of those situations that have inspired me and use them to inspire you. I share all of these experiences in the hope of providing motivation, knowledge, and practical tips for others who find themselves or wish to find themselves on the journey from being average and ordinary to becoming a high achiever.

Part I:
The Mental Matrix

The Mental Matrix is the beginning of mindset development. This section will teach you the full process of thought and how that thinking affects your state, habits, and actions, and leads you to either prosperity or poverty.

– Chapter 1 –

A Ghetto Kid
from New York City

In order to know
why I believe in the concept of mastering the mind,
you must first know
what my mind once believed.

Every Sunday night, I usually hang out in a pair of sweats and a T-shirt, doing a whole lot of nothing. Sunday is family day for me, which means I don't do much. Basically, my wife says no work! If we are not out as a family, we are usually in the bed, watching a movie. This particular Sunday, both my wife and I were on our laptops, watching videos online. I remember I was watching a video that told the history of New York City and some of the iconic landmarks, like the World Trade Center building, Times Square, and the Empire State Building.

Then the video proceeded to talk about some of the extremely rough neighborhoods and how the gaps that separate the "haves" and the "have nots" are not that large. In most areas, this separation is represented by only a few blocks. Watching this brought back so many memories of the years I spent there. It reminded me that I grew up in the land of the "have nots," and as I sat there watching that video, I shed a tear. It reminded me of those days I spent there, hoping to one day cross over to the side of the "haves," where it seemed there were no worries.

Now don't get me wrong, we were not so poor that we didn't eat. My mom, who basically for most of my early childhood was a strong single mom, worked hard to keep food in our bellies, a roof over our heads, and clothes on our backs. She gave up a lot of her own happiness and fun, and most of her life was dedicated to her kids. She taught me one of the biggest life lessons ever, which was the ability to sacrifice the short-term pain for long-term gain. That lesson is very evident in my journey to success throughout my life. Though she worked hard as a single parent, we were surviving but not thriving, and my ambition was always to thrive. I wanted to have and do more than what was available to me. I always had a hunger to blaze a path for myself, my family, and my future family. I wanted to live a life that mattered; I wanted my mom to never have to worry about anything; and I wanted my future family to never have to experience the things that I had to endure in life.

We lived most of our lives in various apartment complexes in Queens, New York. Most of them were not too far from Jamaica Avenue. Growing up, I spent my weeks in Queens and my summers and some weekends in Brownsville, Brooklyn, with my cousins and aunts. Anyone who understands these two areas knows they are not the safest places in the world to live. As a kid, there is a lot of peer pressure to be, think, and behave the way the neighborhood dictated. Out of social pressure and maybe a bit of necessity, I emulated what I saw in the environment. Let's just say I got into some trouble as a kid. I was always a good kid, but I always found myself in places or with people who were not as good. I don't want to make it seem like it was the other kids and not me, because I might not have started the trouble, but I was a part of it.

I remember getting caught bringing a knife to school once, and the principal called my mother. My mother had to leave work and come to my school. That principal then went on to tell my mother that her son would be dead or in jail before the age of 21. Now when most people hear that, they say, "How dare this teacher overstep their boundaries as an educator and say something like that?" Trust me, my mom felt the same way and vehemently disagreed with her.

SACRIFICE THE SHORT - TERM PAIN FOR LONG - TERM GAIN

#TheMentalPlaybook
#MentalAsset

What was worse about that situation is that I believed her, and I went on to live my teenage life with the mentality that I probably would die or be in jail. It wasn't that far-fetched of an idea for me to become a statistic. I had friends and family members go to jail and/or die from getting into a gang beef or just being in the wrong place at the wrong time. It wasn't outlandish to think I would get caught up with the wrong people at the wrong time and end up paying the price for it.

Those comments from that principal would live with me for many years. In those years, I was around drugs, gangs, alcohol, sex, guns, and a lot of things you would probably not want a teenager to be around. I remember the first time I saw a gun. I was about 11 years old, and a guy named Tim (not his real name) pulled out a gun to show me. For some reason, I wasn't scared but more fascinated with it. A part of me wanted my life to go down the path of being a statistic because I felt rebellious. Some of that rebellion came from me being angry because of not having my father in my life the way I would have liked to. From that age to about 18, I lived in that environment and became a product of it. Thank God for a strong mother who did her best to keep me off the streets. She would slap me up for coming home smelling like weed, being out too late, or not staying on top of my school work. Even though I was a kid who got into a bit of trouble, I always knew how to play the game. I realized early that if my mom saw good grades, she would let me go outside without any problems. Because of that, I always tried to keep my grades up so that she never stopped me from going out with the guys or to my cousin's house in Brooklyn. I thought this was me getting what I wanted, but it would be one of the best decisions I made, because my friends didn't do the same. They were all not doing well in school, and they were disrespectful to the teachers and parents in the neighborhood. I did the exact opposite because I hated being on punishment, and I hated being disrespected, so I tried to never disrespect others. Being on punishment just wasn't an option for me because I hated being told that I couldn't do something. At the time, I didn't realize that not liking to be told what to do or the feeling of being bossed around was the beginning mindset of an entrepreneur.

THE HIGH SCHOOL DIPLOMA

It is funny how decisions you make in life don't make sense moving forward but make all the sense in the world when you connect the dots backward. The decision to keep my grades up and always be as respectful as possible so no one could speak ill of me to my mom ended up helping out a lot later in life. Looking back, one of the main reasons I tried to stay out of as much trouble as possible was because I witnessed my mom going through abusive relationships with men, and I didn't want to be another man in her life who let her down.

I remember one of the toughest days of my life. It was the first time I knew for a fact that I had let my mom down big time. It was the first day of the last semester of my senior year at Park West High School, and I had just received my schedule. I remember feeling so excited when I got that schedule because I was on the path to graduating from high school.

Now that might not sound like a big deal to you, but most of my friends and a lot of my family had either dropped out of their schools, gotten kicked out, gone to jail, or died, so this was a big deal for me. That afternoon, we went to shoot hoops, and we got a bright idea to go and steal bikes. This was a common occurrence among kids in my neighborhood. Just a week before that, we had decided that we would not steal any more bikes because we had stolen so many that we didn't want to push our luck. Normally we would steal bikes for a means of transportation or to sell, and since none of our moms would allow us to bring a bike into our small apartments, most times, if we couldn't sell them, we would ditch them at parties.

As we played basketball that day, a friend of a friend came to the court and said he knew where we could steal some high-end bikes to sell. The place he knew was in an all-white neighborhood. Now, as black teenagers riding our bikes around a predominately white neighborhood, you know we stuck out like a sore thumb. We were in a park, and this kid in a light-blue T-shirt had a racing bike that we knew was worth a few hundred, if not a thousand, dollars. Let's just say things escalated quickly, and a gun was drawn to get the bike from this kid so we could get the bike and flee the scene.

Well, because we were silly kids, we stopped in another park some seven blocks away so that some of my friends could have a smoke. Next thing you know, what looked like the entire police department drove down to the park and surrounded us. It was at least 30 police cars, vans, and a helicopter that came down this one-lane road toward the back of the park. Most of us knew there was no getting away from this, but one of my friends, Vince (not his real name), took off. The cops and the helicopters were chasing him for what felt like 10 to 15 minutes. While this was going on, we were being asked to put our hands on the fence while they searched us.

We could literally hear the officers on the police scanner say, "We can't find him. Where did he go?" Some of my friends were screaming, "Yeah! Run, Vince, run!" Some of the officers were yelling at us to be quiet. Toward the end of this manhunt, Vince got caught because he hid behind a garbage can behind a random house. A man walked out of the house, wearing house slippers and a bathrobe, and Vince put his finger to his lips to tell the guy not to say anything. The guy in the bathrobe then pulled out a gun from behind his back and told Vince to get on the ground. Come to find out, Vince hid behind the wrong house, because the guy in the bathrobe, the guy who owned the house, was an undercover cop. Recalling it now, it all seems like a scene out of an action thriller, but at the time, these stories were normal.

They took us all to the precinct and locked us in handcuffs for hours to question us. They individually asked us who was the owner of the gun, and we all pretended not to know about any weapon. All of our stories were the same, and the cops were getting annoyed, but none of us snitched. Where we are from, the cops were the last thing you had to worry about if you snitched. Since we were underage—I was 17 at the time—they said they would call our parents. I can't tell you how much I hated the sound of that. As they put me in the cell and shut the door, I instantly felt the weight of the situation. I sat on the cold bench. I couldn't help but think about earlier that morning, how excited I was about feeling like I would be the one to graduate from high school, and now it looked like all of that excitement got flushed down the toilet. I would in fact be just like everyone else and not make it out of high school. A few hours later, my mom came to the precinct to pick me up, and the look she had on her face broke my spirit. In this moment, I felt like every other man who disappointed her in life. At the time, I wasn't a religious kid. As a matter a fact, I don't think I ever even attended a church service in my life. But I remember praying and saying, "God, if you get me out of this, I will turn it around." At the end of the day, Vince decided to take all the blame, and he went to jail for two years. The officer told me that if one person didn't take the blame, we all would have gone to jail. I tear up thinking about it now: If Vince wouldn't have taken the blame, I would have spent two years of my life in jail over a bike. My life today would be totally different if that one thing changed.

That was a defining moment in my life, where I knew I didn't want to be a statistic and I wanted something more for myself. Though I saw that this wasn't the way I wanted to live, it was difficult to change while being in an environment that didn't allow for that type of growth. Not having opportunities to get out kept me stuck. Even though I wanted to change at the moment, 100 percent, I didn't. I did end up graduating that year, and it was one of the most exciting times of my life. Not only that but my grades were good enough to get me into college. It wasn't until that incident that I knew I absolutely needed to go to college. I ended up going to City College of New York on 138th Street and Convent Avenue in Harlem, the school of alumni like Colin Powell, Henry Kissinger, and Russell Simmons. I was excited and felt like this maybe was a new start for me to turn over a new leaf and be a better person. Instead, I went to school and, at night, kept doing the same things I was doing in the past. What I know now is that no matter how much a person wants to change, without an environment to foster that change, it is highly unlikely change will happen.

THE TRAIN RIDE

The second defining moment in my life happened when I was in college and on the train, headed home. I was with my friends Nick and Johnathan, who I knew from the basketball team at City College. We all were on the E train, riding back toward Queens. I was sitting on one side of the train bench, and Nick and

Johnathan were sitting on the other. I remember it like it was yesterday. We were all wearing our big North Face coats for the winter. As we were sitting there, I remembered that a few days earlier, Johnathan said he knew of a way for me to make an extra few hundred dollars a month, but he never told me what it was. I remember saying to him, "Hey, Johnathan, what's that extra money thing you were talking to me about?" Johnathan and Nick, clearly both "in" on what was happening, started laughing and saying, "Oh, you are not serious!" Being confused, I asked, "Serious about what?" Then Nick said, "About making money." So I asked, "What is it?" They started laughing again. At that moment, I got a bit annoyed and wanted answers. Johnathan said, "I will call you on Saturday, and we will talk about it." Then Johnathan got off the train at his stop. I continued to ask Nick, but he would not budge on the information.

Being so curious, I was mad that they wouldn't tell me right then and there. They made all these excuses about why they couldn't tell me. Though upset, I was still curious, so Saturday rolled around and I was just waiting and waiting for the call. Johnathan didn't call me at the time he said he would, so I called him. "Johnathan, you were supposed to call me. What happened?" He said he forgot, but he had something for me to listen to, and it would explain everything. He let me listen to a prerecorded call that talked about the business, and to be honest, it was so boring that I lost my curiosity. I wasn't really paying attention until the recording said you can make $5,000 a month from home, and my ears perked back up.

At the end of the call, I said to Johnathan, "Okay, so what now?" He said the next step was to talk to Mr. Loubier, and he could answer any questions I had about the business. I got on the phone with Mr. Loubier, and he answered none of my questions about the business but proceeded to invite me to a business meeting at a hotel across the street from Madison Square Garden, called the Hotel Pennsylvania. At this point, you must be saying the same thing I was saying: This all sounds very sketchy. But I trusted Nick and Johnathan, so I went with it. Johnathan assured me that he would be at the event, so I decided to go because I knew I wouldn't be alone. I was also supposed to meet this "Mr. Loubier" character at the event, and I was guessing that he was going to interview me or something.

I got dressed up in a bubble jacket, my stepfather's tie, and his dress shirt. My stepfather is about 5'5" and I am 6'2", so obviously his shirt didn't fit and the sleeves didn't go past my forearms, which is why I never took off my coat. I also wore some slacks and shoes from my high school prom. I was uncomfortable all the way around because I was wearing clothes I didn't normally wear and I was on the train going to a hotel at 7:00 p.m. for a business meeting that sounded super sketchy. On top of that, when I got there, I called Johnathan and he said that he couldn't make it. I literally hung up the phone and started making my way to the exit. I got to the lobby, and all of a sudden, I saw a familiar face.

It was a friend named Michael, who also played ball on the team, but I never really talked to him. Up until that point, there were only five words we had said to each other for months. At the end of basketball practice, we would both stay after to get some shots up. Mike would be on one end of the full court, and I would be on the other. Whenever one of us was on the way out, I would say, "Mad Mike" (because he had mad skills on the court), and he would say, "Eugene the Dream." Those were literally the only words we said to each other for months. When I saw him at the sketchy hotel at 7:00 p.m., I felt a bit relieved to see a familiar face in the crowd. I went to say what's up and ask him what he was doing at the hotel, and he said he was going to the same event I was. I said, "What a coincidence. That's super cool because I was supposed to go to this event with Johnathan, but he flaked on me." Mike said, "It's cool. You can go in with me." We started talking as we walked to the registration table to get our name tags.

The place was packed with a few hundred people in the halls, all wearing beautiful dresses or nice suits and ties. It was so hard to get through the hall to the registration table, but we both finally got there and got our name tags. We started talking again, waiting for the doors to open. Then, in mid-sentence, I looked down at Mike's name tag, and it read "Mr. Loubier." Now I was super confused. I said, "Wait, Mike, you were the guy I was talking to on the phone?" Mike laughed so hard and said, "Yes, that was me." I just started laughing so hard because I was so confused about the whole ordeal. I was also very curious because, in my mind, all I could think was, if they went through all of this to get me to come to this event, then it must be something good. What also had me curious was that this place was packed with smiling people. If you know New York, you know people don't smile much there, so I knew something good had to be going on.

I sat in the room, and a gentleman by the name of Obinna Ndu started to speak on the stage. This guy was masterful with his words, the best I had ever seen. This was the first time I ever thought about being a public speaker because I was amazed at how he mystified the crowd with every word. As I sat there, I watched this man like a hawk. I never checked out a guy so hard in my life. I watched his facial expressions. I looked at his clothes and his shoes. He looked clean and put together. He looked like a million bucks, and in that moment, I believed what he was saying. About 20 minutes into his presentation, he started talking about the money you can make with the business, and

I said to myself, "Man, I am in! Where is the paperwork?"

After the event, they handed over the paperwork, and it was $249 to join this business. I immediately thought, "Well I don't have $249, but I will find it!" They had me fill out the paperwork and leave the payment part blank. I can't remember what excuse I gave them for why I didn't have my bank card. As I sat there a few minutes, the negative mentality that had been programmed into me as a kid started coming up. I started to think back to that principal who said I would be dead or in jail before 21. I started thinking about the fact that I should be a statistic. My mind said, "Who am I to think I can be successful? Look at where I come from. Look at how I look!" I saw these guys with suits and nice cars, and I just felt like this ghetto kid from New York City who had no chance of making it in business.

After the event, Mike offered to pay for dinner, and being a broke college student, I said, "YES!!" We went out to Chevys, and a guy by the name of Ed Wagaba went with us. As we got there, in my mind, I was thinking, "Man, I am not good enough. This success stuff seems like it won't be my reality." As we ate, Ed and Mike were having a good time laughing and joking, which made me relax and have a good time myself. Something I realized in that moment was that these guys were regular people just like me. Then the words of the speaker on the stage popped into my mind. He said, "If we can do it, why not you? And if you think you can't, then what you say to yourself becomes your reality." I decided in the restaurant that I was going to do the business. Little did I know that this decision would change the course of my life.

THE ROAD TRIP

About two weeks after getting started with the company, I was on a conference call with Mike, and I heard people talking about the fact that everyone in the company was going to Oklahoma. They said that everyone making $10,000 a month or more would be at this event. I must say that caught my attention, but I thought to myself, "That's cool that they are all going there, but I am not going! One, I don't have the money to go, and two, at 18 years old, I have never even left the state of New York before except when I went to Disneyland when I was six." The next day, I saw Mike in school, and he asked me if I was going to Oklahoma. I told him no, that I had class, that I had to worry about my mom not letting me, and that I didn't have money. After about 30 minutes of convincing me I should go, he offered to give up his plane ticket and drive there with me. I finally said yes, used my school loan check that I was supposed to use for school books, and registered for the event.

The day of this road trip, Mike, Nick, and I were in the parked rental car outside of City College of New York. I was sitting in the front seat, and Mike asked me to pass him the map in the glove compartment. Yes, these were the days when you had to print out maps and it wasn't on your phone. I pulled the map out, and it said Oklahoma was 24 hours from New York. Now forgive me, but I always used to sleep in geography class. I did not know Oklahoma was 24 hours away. I almost got out of the car right then and there, but I didn't. As we drove down, they listened to a guy by the name of Jim Rohn. Keep in mind, I am new to all of this, so I didn't know what personal development was. All I knew was that these guys liked listening to it. At the time, I was heavily into music, and I was listening to my own album that I was creating. I remember taking my headphones off about eight hours into the trip and couldn't believe these guys were still listening to this Jim Rohn guy. I immediately put my headphones back on and thought to myself that these guys were crazy to listen to a guy talk for hours.

We got to Oklahoma, and Nick stepped out of the car and started screaming, "Wooooo!" I asked him why he was so excited to go to Oklahoma when there was nothing but cows and tumbleweeds. I just didn't understand these guys at the time. Little did I know, I was headed for another life-defining moment. I went to this event where there were over 15,000 people excited to learn from millionaires. I couldn't help being swept up in the excitement. It didn't matter that I came there on my last dime, and it didn't matter that it was seven guys staying in our one hotel room. It didn't even matter that we were eating peanut butter sandwiches because we couldn't afford the jelly. At that moment, all I felt was euphoria. I remember sitting way up in the nosebleed section, and a guy by the name of Darnell Self got onstage. Now, Darnell was between 30 to 35 years of age. He is African American. He grew up in the type of neighborhood I did, and he was at the top of the company. This was the one time I saw someone who was successful that didn't sell drugs, play sports, or make music. He spoke about Harriet Tubman and the Underground Railroad in relation to setting people free in business. He was another speaker who just captivated the audience, and I saw myself in him. I related to him. This was the first time I saw myself living past 21 years old. This was the first time I started to see myself as more than the ghetto kid from New York. At that event, I also went to a church service for the first time, and that weekend, I found faith.

On the trip back to New York City, I felt like a new person. I was unstoppable. I felt like my life would never be the same. This event shifted the way I looked at life. I didn't know it then, but I know now, that this weekend was when I mentally shifted from believing that I was less than to believing that I could concur the world. On the drive back, they were listening to the Jim Rohn guy again, and I thought, wow, now I get why you could listen to this guy for hours. I couldn't get enough. I listened to him the whole way back. I basically got dragged on this road trip, and it literally changed my life mentally, spiritually, and emotionally. On the outside, I was the same person, but on the inside, my mind changed. It was like I was living a programmed life before, and the blinders were removed from my eyes. I was determined to take this new mindset and change my life forever.

I tell you all these stories to give you a glance into the beginning of my journey in turning my mind into an asset for me instead of a liability. It's also to show you that we all are faced with the task of growing our thinking in a way that will serve us. I was once a lost ghetto kid from New York. I went from believing my principal's negative words and dealing with living in an impoverished neighborhood to going on a road trip where everything changed for me. This was the beginning of my life turning around for the better. This is when I began to understand and believe that if you can change the way you think, then you can change the game in your life.

– Chapter 2 –

Now the Journey
Really Begins

*When you're an amateur,
you think success should
happen quickly.*

Now that I had come back to New York a new man, you would think that it was all success from there. The journey of changing your mindset starts with changing your thought patterns. I didn't realize that this shift in mindset meant not only having new philosophies but using those philosophies to dictate my actions. My belief is that you really haven't shifted your mindset until that new philosophy is acted out in the times when you are tested. If I had to choose my philosophy, it is that when bad situations happen, I respond instead of reacting. That sounds great, but to me, it's not your philosophy unless, when a situation arises that could be handled in a reaction, you decide to respond. So many people can recite sections in books—they can memorize quotes—but when it comes to living the quotes, they simply don't.

This is where I found myself when I came back to New York. I learned some great philosophies, but I hadn't learned how to make the philosophies more than just words. I learned all of this great stuff, and I thought I should now be successful right away. When you're an amateur, you think success should happen quickly. I didn't realize the hard work and dedication that came with life change at the time, but I sure did learn it. I really learned it as I came into the understanding of what I call the Mental Matrix. As I mentioned in the introduction, this book will be broken up into two sections. In the first section, I will present to you a concept called the Mental Matrix, which I have been studying and using since I was 18 years old. The Mental Matrix is the beginning framework of understanding how the mind works in relation to creating success. Then in the second section of the book, I will present to you 10 key ways to think that separate the average from the high achiever and some practical strategies and stories that you can learn from immediately and apply in your life.

When I was 18 and just coming back from Oklahoma City, I realized that there was more to this success thing than just wanting it. I started to pick up clues from trainings, books, seminars, and mentors. Through learning and developing, I put together the simple and practical pieces of the Mental Matrix. The Mental Matrix will do a few things for you:

- It will give you practical steps to mastering the mind and shifting your mental perspective.

- It will teach you how to think like an ultimate high achiever.
- It will help you learn how your thoughts, mind, and body are all connected and how each of them work together to affect your results.
- And it will show you how to create success on demand at any moment and any time.

I believe that understanding the Mental Matrix, when it comes to mastering the mind and turning your mind into an asset instead of a liability, will take you to unprecedented heights. That's enough buildup. So what is the Mental Matrix? It is the framework in the image you see below.

The Mental Matrix

This framework has multiple parts, and I will try to break down each part into its simplest form. Let's start with the top half of the Mental Matrix. When it comes to success, there are two mental phases we control in our mind at all times. Those two phases are fear and faith. The way we think dictates which one of those phases controls our state, actions, and habits either negatively or positively.

MENTAL MATRIX

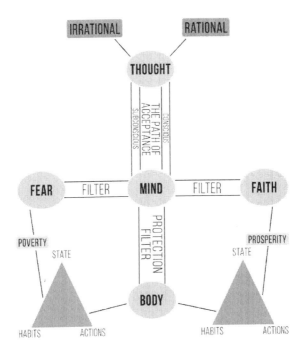

The question I usually get when I make that statement is, "If we know that in success we control the two mental phases of fear and faith, and we also know that the way we think dictates our state, actions, and habits, then what dictates the way we think?" The reason that's such a good question is, if you can figure out what dictates your thinking, then you can reverse engineer the entire process.

Back when I was still a teenager, the question of what dictates thinking used to keep me up at night. My mentor used to say all the time that if you can change the way you think, you can succeed in anything. I wanted to find out how to change my thinking in such a way that success was possible for me. I spent money, time, and energy trying to learn from everyone I could to put the pieces of this Mental Matrix together. I wanted to know what makes a person think the way they do. What does it take to change the way a person thinks? How can you take a change of mindset and turn it into a change in lifestyle?

Thoughts

After years of studying and hundreds of thousands of dollars spent paying for seminars, trainings, and traveling the globe to learn from the of the world, I have concluded that thinking is simply the practice of two things:

1) Asking questions
2) Answering questions

The way a person thinks is in large measure the questions they ask themselves internally and the way they answer those same questions. I will come back to asking and answering questions, but let me go back to the thinking for a second. The average person has between 35 and 48 thoughts a minute. That's over 50,000 to 70,000 thoughts a day. Each thought either puts you in a state (an emotion or feeling) or makes you take an action.

For Example:

> I am hungry. – This is a state.
> I started eating. – This is an action.

> My arm itches. – This is a state.
> I scratched my arm. – This is an action.

> I am thirsty. – This is a state.
> I drank a glass of water. – This is an action.

THINKING
IS SIMPLY THE
PRACTICE
OF 2
THINGS

1)ASKING
QUESTIONS

2)ANSWERING
QUESTIONS

#TheMentalPlaybook
#MentalAsset

Your mind is constantly processing thoughts to take actions or put you in a specific state or feeling, especially when it comes to achievement. Your mind is processing these thoughts, and they can drive you to either negative or positive responses. I stated earlier that thinking is the practice of answering and asking questions, but what dictates whether those thoughts are positive or negative? The answer to that question is in whether those questions and answers are empowering or disempowering.

For clarity's sake, let me break this down one more time. The process of thinking is asking and answering questions. When thinking, the thoughts put you in a specific state or make you take an action. When your mind processes that thought, it will either be processed negatively or positively. When you think, you are basically asking and answering questions, and whether those questions are negative or positive is determined by whether they are empowering or disempowering. If you can understand this, then this is where revolutionary change starts because you can dictate your results when you learn to properly filter your questions and answers.

I remember, a few years back, I went to a Tony Robbins event, and there were thousands of people in the room. The event was buzzing with excitement, and I remember Tony coming onstage and saying something that I thought was huge. He said, "You can control your life when you control the questions you ask yourself." I believe this 100 percent. I believe you can control your life, your results, your happiness, your finances, and your body. You can control everything in your life when you control your questions. When it comes to empowering and disempowering questions, usually people either don't know or don't realize when they are doing either.

Disempowering Questions:
- Why me?
- Why can't I do this?
- Why am I so (insert negative thought)?
- What if I can't do it?
- What's wrong with me?
- Why can't I make more money or lose weight?

<u>Empowering Questions:</u>

-   How can I make this work?
-   What can I do to win?
-   Why am I so (insert positive thought)?
-   How can I resolve this?
-   How can I add more value?

When you ask disempowering questions, you feel helpless, hopeless, victimized, and overwhelmed. All of these feelings cause you to take negative actions, like judging people, being controlling, or being mean. When you ask empowering questions, you feel uplifted, resourceful, energetic, and optimistic. All of these feelings cause you to take positive actions, like looking for solutions, cooperating, or shifting your focus to things you can control.

When we ask ourselves empowering questions, our rational brain takes over. Rational thinking focuses on logic and reason which forces conscious thinking. When we ask disempowering questions, our irrational brain takes over, and irrational thinking has no logic or reasoning and is tied to subconscious thinking. I will talk more about conscious and subconscious in a second, but the main point is that if you are asking empowering questions, it forces you to take time and process answers though logic and reason.

One of the best ways to ask empowering questions is to make them open-ended questions. An open-ended question forces you to formulate an answer that is more thoughtful than just yes or no. For example, if you ask yourself a question like, "Am I good enough?" this is not an open-ended question; it's a direct question. If you are currently a negative person, your subconscious will answer directly with a yes or no based on how it has been answered in the past. A better question is, "What do I need to do to be good enough?" That open-ended question forces the mind to think rationally to find an acceptable answer. In doing this, your chances of getting an empowering answer increase drastically.

Now it is still possible to ask an open-ended question, think logically, and still get a disempowering answer. I will explain how that's possible in a later chapter, but rational thinking and irrational thinking can both create success in your life if you develop the proper habits. Actually, training your irrational thinking is one of the biggest causes of success and failure.

The process of learning all this is the journey I found myself on and the journey you will likely find yourself on—the journey of shifting your thoughts into ones that will support your desires to become a high achiever—and this process doesn't happen overnight. I thought after learning this concept that if I asked and answered questions in an empowering way, then I would always take the right actions, always be in the right state, and always have positive habits that would lead me to abundance and prosperity. Here was my problem though: By the time I learned all these principles, I was 20 years old and already had 20 years of those negative downloads in my head. In today's society, it is rare to see or hear empowering words or situations. You turn on the TV today, and you hear about fires, shootings, back-biting, anger, financial crisis, and war. If that is being poured into your head every day for 20 years, it is easy to see how a person could build a habit of negativity.

Reprogramming

The great thing is that you can reprogram the years of negativity into positivity. Any habit you currently have can be reprogrammed into a habit that serves you. Most people believe that habits are nearly impossible to remove, but quite frankly, it's the exact opposite. Habits are actually pretty simple to reprogram. The key is to focus your constant awareness of the habit you want to change. For example, when I was 18, I cursed about five times per sentence. I *literally* could not say a full sentence without dropping an "F-bomb." I wanted to stop cursing because I started going to church and also because I started in business. I thought to myself that it was bad enough that I didn't look very professional, but the least I could do was sound professional. That task was definitely easier said than done.

The thing that allowed me to reprogram that habit was a heightened sense of curse words. My awareness was high, and I paid very close attention when I heard it. Even when I heard someone else say it, I would remind myself that I couldn't curse. In the beginning, it was extremely tough. I would curse and catch the fact that I would curse every once in a while.

Then, because of my heightened focus, I would catch it right after I said a curse word. Then I got the magic idea of putting a rubber band on my wrist, and every time I cursed and caught it, I would pull the rubber band back and let it pop my wrist. This negative enforcement plus the heighted awareness helped me start to reprogram this habit. I started catching myself right before the curse word came out of my mouth. I cut the cursing down from multiple times a sentence to a few times a day to once in a day or every other day and then every few months. Slowly but surely, the cursing stopped altogether. I was fully reprogrammed by awareness. Another way to think of awareness is to be "conscious." The key to my ability to reprogram myself was my ability to now be conscious of what I wanted and didn't want.

Learning to focus on your conscious and subconscious brain is key to reprogramming but also learning how your conscious and subconscious brain asks and answers the questions you think. Let me try and break down the conscious and subconscious in its simplest form. Your mind requires a lot of energy to operate, especially when you have to think rationally.

Problem-solving or making decisions takes a ton of brain energy, and it's a bit of a slower process. What your mind does is look for ways to be more efficient with that energy. One way it does this is through conscious and subconscious processing. Our minds are constantly looking for ways to automate these processes to save time and brain energy. This process is called subconscious thinking. This takes care of basic life functions, like fight-or-flight and, more importantly, our learned behavior and habits.

Our subconscious also records our past experiences and knowledge. This is what memory is developed from, storing it in our minds like photos in a picture album. The state we felt in these pictures forms a frame around the photos, which gives things meaning for us. Whether it's giving us meaning for people, objects, and events, over time this framing develops our attitudes to become either positive or negative. This is why it is very important to be very mindful of the meaning we give things that happen in our life. If every time you have an experience that is not the one you want and you frame all these situations as negative experience, over time you will have way more negative experiences than positive ones.

Our subconscious controls our daily decision-making that impacts our daily habits. Your habits could be one of the biggest stumbling blocks to living a life of abundance and prosperity, and those habits are dictated by your subconscious. Conscious thinking is a rational action that forces our brains to use logic and reason to make decisions. Conscious thinking gives us the opportunity to choose empowering or disempowering answers when asking questions. This is opposed to subconscious thinking that is operating on habits. These habits have been created over time by your conscious mind's consistent decisions. The good news is, the same way your conscious mind programmed your subconscious to create your habits, you can use this same processes to change the bad habits into habits that serve your goals and dreams.

The great thing about the Mental Matrix is that it all starts with thoughts, and thoughts are something that you can control. Once a thought comes into your mind by the questions it asks and answers, those questions and answers will be filtered by your subconscious or conscious, which will determine a rational or irrational response. That thought is now sent through what I call the path of acceptance to the mind. Conscious thoughts and subconscious thoughts can both be filtered through the path of acceptance. When a thought goes through the path of acceptance from your conscious mind, you have consciously made the decision to accept that thought and allow it to pass through. When a thought goes through the path of acceptance from your subconscious mind, you have not made the conscious decision to accept that thought, but that thought is accepted based on the habits you have allowed.

The path of acceptance leads to the next section of the Mental Matrix, which is the mind, my favorite section of this framework. The journey of understanding thought and knowing how to think is not easy, especially in the beginning phases of learning. The quicker you allow yourself to accept that learning this process is where your journey begins, the quicker you will be able to move closer to higher levels of achieve-ment.

The Mind:
The Psychological Process

*If you change the way you
look at things, the way you
look at things will change.*

The fact that the mind has untold power is not really a new concept, yet very few people tap into this power to create the life they truly want. The question is, why? When you look at the mind and you compare it to the most powerful thing a human has created, the computer, there is no real comparison. If you take a computer in today's time (which I am sure if you are reading this book 10 or 20 years from now, these numbers may be off but not the concept), it can hold 250,000 pictures, 20,000 songs, and hundreds of full-length movies, and we fit all those things on a thumb drive. Now if we compare it to the mind, it can hold 10,000,000,000,000,000 operations per second without your own conscious knowledge of it. Your mind can push blood through your veins at the perfect pressure; it can keep your heart beating 24 hours a day, seven days a week. It can also keep your body's core temperature at the perfect rate to keep you alive, and this is just the tip of the iceberg.

Once again, why don't people turn to the mind to create the life they deserve? When things are not going right in a person's life, when their goals seem far away, when they feel like they are in a pit of despair, why don't they look at the way they think as a solution to the problems? I have come to realize that most times the reason is because people just don't know that the way they think is a factor. This book was created for that very reason, to help people see that just the smallest mental shift can make a huge difference in their confidence, self-esteem, finances, career, happiness, and so much more.

Some people might even ask, based on that last statement, "Come on, Eugene, a shift in your mind will change your emotional state?" My answer to that is absolutely. If you are in the office, not having a good day, but then you get news that you just won 2 million in the lottery, how would you feel? You would be excited, jumping up and down, and very happy. Well just minutes before, you were having a bad day. The only thing that changed was your mental state because the news of winning the lottery was greater than your annoyance of being at work. Now let's say an hour later, you get a message that someone extremely close to you has died—now how do you feel? You feel extremely miserable, sad, depressed, and mopey, and are probably crying. You just went from extreme happiness to tears in an instant. You never changed location; you are still at your job; and you never changed anything around you. The only things that changed were the things that went into your mind and shifted how you felt, your body language and your happiness.

What most people don't understand is that the mind and the body are one.

MENTAL MATRIX

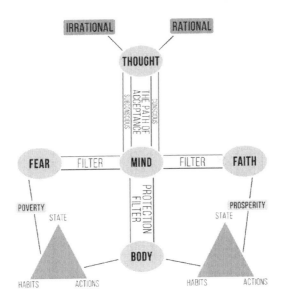

When the mind processes a thought, it goes through what I like to call the protection filter. This is where the mind tells the body how to respond to the thought to protect the body from any danger whether emotional or physical. Once the body gets this thought from the mind, it instantaneously creates either a negative or positive state, action, or habit. If it creates a positive state, action, or habit, it leads a person to prosperity, which operates on the mental side of faith. If it creates a negative state, action, or habit, it leads a person into poverty, which operates on the mental side of fear.

By the way, when I say prosperity, I am not just talking financially. Prosperity is when your life is flourishing, thriving, and successful. The same with poverty, it's not just lack of money; it's the state of being inferior in quality or insufficient in amount. This can be an insufficient amount of money, love, happiness, peace, abundance, etc. Later in the book, I will talk about how all of these things come together.

Going back to the mind, there is a pillar of the mind that I like to call the psychological process. I call it this because all success starts in the mind. Before we can talk about success, abundance, or prosperity, we have to first study the mind. Will your thinking allow you to achieve the success desired? Just like a mechanic would go under the hood of a car and examine the engine for optimal driving success, I want to do the same for your mindset. I want you to metaphorically open up the hood of your head, examine the engine called your brain, and get it working at optimal strength. I want to talk about the five phases of the psychological processes.

Phase 1: The Awareness Phase

Awareness allows you to understand the environment around you and process that data. Processing the data allows you to take action on that data in the near or distant future. Awareness is dictated by our five senses, and through those senses, we gain clarity about the world around us. The awareness phase is the process of seeing, hearing, touching, smelling, or feeling the world around you. Outside of the five senses, there are things that effect awareness, like temperature, pain, motion, and pressure.

There Are Two Types of Awareness:

1) **World Awareness:** World awareness has the power of influence. It influences what you see, how you see it, what you hear, and what you take in. From a psychological perspective, it's important to consciously control your worldview. Though you may be aware of what is happening around you, you do not allow the worldview to dictate how you think or how you process thoughts. You must have

more of an impact on the world than the world has on you.

2) **Self-Awareness:** Self-awareness is the process of understanding ourselves. If world awareness is about understanding and gaining clarity of the world around us, then self-awareness is about gaining clarity and understanding the world within us. Most people are not aware of who they really are, and they can't even articulate their own character, skills, motives, and desires. This lack of awareness is the reason so many are so far from what they would call success. When you are not clear about who you are, you are not clear about what to do, and if you are not clear about what to do, you are not clear about who you should become. When you are not clear about who you should become, you stay who you are.

Having world awareness and self-awareness is very important, but if you feel like you are lacking in that area, what do you do? How do you increase your awareness? There are three things you should focus on if you want to increase your awareness.

Increasing Your Awareness

1) **Get Clarity on Who You Are:** When you are clear about who you are, the world can't dictate how you think. Getting clarity on who you are is not about being perfect; it's loving yourself and keeping other people's opinions out of your head.

2) **Be Attentive:** Many times, we live life by going through the motions. Going through the motions is something we can't do if we want success because if our subconscious is not trained, it will lead us to do things and think thoughts that don't serve us.

3) **Be Present:** Being present gives you energy, and where your awareness goes, your energy flows. Most people are tuned into the radio station WINFM: What's In It For ME? Even when people are talking to others, they can't be present in the conversation because they are focused on themselves and what they are about to say. Being present also means taking care of yourself. Being present is tough when you lack the energy and you are fatigued. Taking care of your body will give you the

energy you need to interact with the world on a higher level.

Phase 2: Perception

The second of the five phases of the psychological processes is perception. Perception is such a big topic that I could do a whole book on it. My opinion is that this is one of the huge missing pieces of mental success for most people. Perception is how you interpret what you take in. Your perception is how you see things that are happening around you and what meaning you put to those things you see. Here is the problem with perception with most people: When life happens to a person, which it does to everyone, the meaning they put on that situation is usually disempowering.

They go after success; they fail; and the meaning they put on that situation is that they are not good enough to succeed. That is a perception built by the way you saw that particular failure. There are people who grew up in tough environments, like I did, where they didn't see many success stories, and the meaning they put on it is that people from this neighborhood don't make it. You tried diet after diet, and nothing

PERCEPTION IS HOW YOU INTERPERET WHAT YOU TAKE IN

#TheMentalPlaybook
#MentalAsset

seemed to work, so the way you look at it is that you will never lose weight. These are perceptions that when you see all situations that happen to you as disempowering, it would never be possible to move forward.

They go after success; they fail; and the meaning they put on that situation is that they are not good enough to succeed. That is a perception built by the way you saw that particular failure. There are people who grew up in tough environments, like I did, where they didn't see many success stories, and the meaning they put on it is that people from this neighborhood don't make it. You tried diet after diet, and nothing seemed to work, so the way you look at it is that you will never lose weight. These are perceptions that when you see all situations that happen to you as disempowering, it would never be possible to move forward.

What is your perspective when negativity happens to you? How do you see these things? I remember when I was 19 years old, I was in Vegas at a business convention. During lunch at an In-N-Out, a peer of mine said, "If you change the way you look at things, the way you look at things will change." I never forgot that moment because it made an impact on my life. I realized that I could start seeing the things that were once impossible in my life as possible. This mental shift is responsible for much of the success in my life. Prior to this mental shift, I used to believe that making $2,000 a month was a big deal because most people my age weren't making anything. My perception was in what other people were doing around me, and I had not opened up my horizon to what was possible for me. As I started working on what was possible to make it a reality, I went from earning $10,000 in a year to $10,000 in a month to having weeks and even days where I made over $10,000. The difference in a $10,000 year and a $10,000 day was all perspective in what I saw to be possible.

If I could give you one gift right now, it would be the gift of empowering perception, and guess what, I am going to give you that gift right now because I am going to show you exactly how to shift your perception in an instant. I am going to give you the four keys of perspective shifting. These four keys will give you the things that are most important to perception and changing it.

4 KEYS TO SHIFTING YOUR PERSPECTIVE

You have a choice

Find a mentor

Ask questions

Be patient

Four Keys of Perspective Shifting

1) **Be Aware That You Choose:** When you are a child, your perception of life and what's possible is given to you. As you become a teenager, you start to realize you have the power to change some of the perception you have been given, which is why a lot of teenagers get into a rebellious phase. The

truth of the matter is that, as adults, we usually re-vert back to those childhood perceptions, and if you're not careful, you could be living your life through the perception of the people who raised you. What you must be aware of is that the belief of the success you want and desire is wrapped in your perception of what's possible. Right now, this instant, you can change that perception into an em-powering one. You have the choice, and you can decide. When you come of age to make decisions, one of the decisions you should make is being aware that today you can choose empowering per-ception, and those empowering perceptions can change your life.

2) **Find a Mentor:** It's hard to solve the problem in your own thinking when you are the one who cre-ated the problem in the first place. It's hard to see when you are messing it up yourself. Find a men-tor, a coach—someone who can see what you can't and help you adjust. I remember one of the college basketball coaches from City College of New York, Coach Brad, and he used to say, "Eugene, on the

release of your jump shot, your left hand stays on the ball too long." I never noticed that, but because he was on the outside looking in, he was able to see what I couldn't. Now a lot of people say they can't find a mentor because the people they want to mentor them are not going to do it. Here is a way to get around that. You need to be open to take coaching from people a few steps ahead of you. Here is what I mean: When people usually go for coaches, they normally say they want the top person in that field. Now if you can afford to, you should go learn from that person, but most times, those people are out of reach in the beginning. Yes, you can and should buy and listen to their programs and go to their events, but it's nothing like someone just working right there with you. I also know there is a school of thought that says you should only learn from those who have what you want. I agree with that to an extent, but I also believe you can learn from those who are a few steps ahead of you and are on the journey of having the things you want as well. These people are accessible and may be willing to work with you. That extra mentor help can be very valuable to see what it is you can't.

3) **Ask Questions:** Here is the thing not enough people do, and this is all about taking the time to think. When you hear a perception or perspective from anyone, you must ask yourself if you agree with the assessment. If you do, ask for even more clarity, but if you don't, then don't take it at face value. Always, always, always take the time to think, "Do I really believe this? Is this my perception, or is this the perception of the one I am hearing it from?" Never take on a new philosophy without asking yourself some questions about that philosophy. "Do I really believe this? Is this school of thought empowering? Does this way of thinking align with my core values? If I take on this way of thinking, how will it impact my life? Am I being peer pressured into this way of thinking?" Asking these questions and more can help you develop a habit of being mindful of the philosophies you take in and asking the right questions to make sure you are

shifting your perspective for the positive and not the negative.

4) **Be Patient:** Now this one may seem a little odd to be a key to shifting your perspective, but it is. The lack of patience forces people to rush results, quit, and adopt negative perspectives. The idea of patience is being willing to allow the process to happen in your life. In today's world of technology, it suggests that everything is automated and everything is instant. No one wants to wait and put in the work, and if it looks like work knocking on most people's doors, they think the work has the wrong address. People see the people they admire in places of influence, and they see the glitz and glamour, but they don't see the struggle that they went through to get there. What people want is the riches without the process, but the real riches are the process. The real riches are in the obstacles— that's where you develop tenacity and toughness. Most people never see the test; they only see the testimony. They run to have their own testimony

of greatness, but then they run into a test that con-tradicts the testimony. Through this contradiction, they misidentify the test and say, "That must not be what I am looking for," but in reality, that is ex-actly what they are looking for. Your testimony is in your test; the victory is in your defeat; and the power is in your pain, so if you run from the pain, you run from the power. It takes patience to go through the defeat, the pain, and the test to get to the testimony. Having patience and not rushing success and going through the process will allow you to endure all the way to victory.

Phase 3: Attention

The third of the five phases of the psychologi-cal processes is attention. Most people want success, but they pay attention to the highlights of failures that they have had in life. Where is your attention? I am a big fan of technology—I mean, I run a technology company—but there is one thing I will say technology has done to us, and that one thing is distracting us from the things we go through on a daily basis. Technology is the world's "ADD." For most people today, everything is too slow, not fast enough. Six-second videos are too long; microwaves are too slow; and fast food is not fast enough. I am all for speed and efficiency, but because there is so much speed in the world, the average person's attention span has shrunk. The lack of attention that people pay to the things that are important is sad, and if you want to succeed in life in a big way, you must understand that success is slow. It's a marathon not a sprint. We must not let the speed of life kill our ability to pay attention.

One day, a man named Mr. Success went into a weapons store and met a man behind the counter by the name of Mr. Failure. He said to Mr. Failure, "What is the most powerful weapon you have?" Mr. Failure said, "Let me walk you around the store to show you what I have." He took him to the front counter and showed him a weapon called "Lack of a Plan." He said, "I often use this when I want to throw a person off and have them going in circles with no true purpose." Mr. Success said, "No, I am looking for a stronger weapon than that. What else do you have." Mr. Failure said, "Okay, let's go over here to the back counter and look at one of my all-time favorite weapons. This weapon is called 'Caring what people think.'" Mr. Success said, "Now we are getting closer to what I am looking for, but I want your strongest weapon in the store." Mr. Failure knew exactly what Mr. Success was talking about, so he said, "Come with me. I am going to take you to our secret back room." Mr. Failure went to the back room that was protected by a retinal scan and fingerprinted metal doors into a room that had this one weapon, which was called "Distraction." He said, "I have used distraction to throw even the greatest of achievers off their path, and the thing about distraction is that it is subtle. You can kill them with it before they even realize they are dying."

I tell this story to illustrate that distraction is a powerful thing. This is how powerful distraction is. While you have been reading this book, you have at least once checked your email, picked up your phone, checked your social media, or talked to someone since the start of this chapter. What most people lack is focus. That's what distraction is; it's a shift in focus. Usually it's shifting focus away from what you want and onto what you don't want. Have you ever caught yourself knowing you had work to do, yet 15 to 20 minutes went by because you were scrolling on your phone? Focus can be very difficult because there are so many voices, things, and events that want our attention. So how do you master focus?

There are two basic things you can do today to help you become more focused. The first thing you must do is kill the notifications—the notifications on your phone, computer, or tablet. Just eliminate them. Get rid of the alert when you get an email or a social media notification. You don't need to be dragged to those notifications every time you see them. If you are like me, you get annoyed when you see that notification next to one of your aps. The best thing to do is get rid of them. Here is a practical reason you should kill the notification. If you jump to these notifications every time you see them pop up, then you are on the agenda of the person who sent them instead of your own agenda. You are working on a project; you get a notification; and you stop your project, abandon your agenda, and pick up someone else's. That's distraction; that's lack of attention; and that leads to failure.

The second thing you must do to focus is to eliminate the "shoulds." There are tons of things you should do, but you need to give that up and focus on the things you must do. Like one of my mentors, Tony Robbins, always says, "You don't get in life what you should have. You get in life what you must have." Right now, create a list of 25 goals that you would love to accomplish. Now take five goals out of that 25 that you must accomplish. Now take the other 20 goals and don't even worry about them. Focus all your time and attention on the goals you must have, and when you achieve the ones you must have, you can repeat the exercise again with those remaining 20 if they are still the same goals over that time.

Phase 4: Learning

The fourth of the five phases of the psychological processes is learning. Now this topic I am not going to talk a lot about because I am going to talk more about it later in the book. The reason I have it here is because I want to talk about a specific kind of learning—learning how to think. When most people think about learning, they think about being in a class or reading a book like this, but most never spend any time learning exactly how to think. In success, learning how to think is not a "nice to have"; it's a necessity. This type of learning is not a one-time skill; it is a skill that must be practiced consistently forever. It has taken years for most people to develop negative thinking, and it will take time to shift it to positive.

Traditionally, most are taught what to think instead of how to think. This is something that should be taught in school, but our current educational system is more focused on memorization of the skills instead of the actual learning of skills. Let's not go down that rabbit hole though. Learning to think comes in six stages. I learned this from a professor a few years ago, and it has stuck with me ever since.

6 stages of Learning

Stage 1: The Unreflective Thinker: They are unaware that there is a significant problem in their thinking.

Stage 2: The Challenged Thinker: They are now aware that there are problems in their thinking, but they haven't started making changes.

6 STAGES OF LEARNING

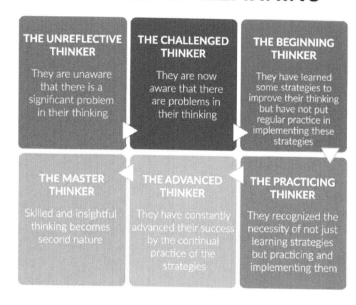

THE UNREFLECTIVE THINKER

They are unaware that there is a significant problem in their thinking

THE CHALLENGED THINKER

They are now aware that there are problems in their thinking

THE BEGINNING THINKER

They have learned some strategies to improve their thinking but have not put regular practice in implementing these strategies

THE MASTER THINKER

Skilled and insightful thinking becomes second nature

THE ADVANCED THINKER

They have constantly advanced their success by the continual practice of the strategies

THE PRACTICING THINKER

They recognized the necessity of not just learning strategies but practicing and implementing them

Stage 3: The Beginning Thinker: They have learned some strategies to improve thinking but are not putting those strategies into regular practice.

Stage 4: The Practicing Thinker: They recognize the necessity of not just learning correct thinking but practicing and implementing them.

Stage 5: The Advanced Thinker: They have advanced because of the continual practice and implementation of correct thinking strategies.

Stage 6: The Master Thinker: Their skilled and insightful thinking has not only become consistent, but it has become second nature.

Stage 6 is where I hope to get you over time with this book and other programs I release. I just believe with all my heart that shifting thinking is the beginning of the highest levels of achievement. There is a very basic way to develop these stages of learning how to think. You must do these three things: 1) accept the fact that there is a problem with your thinking; 2) learn the proper thinking strategies; and 3) commit to the regular practice and implementation of the strategies until they become second nature.

Phase 5: Retention

The fifth and final phase of the five phases of the psychological process is retention. Now what do I mean by this, and why is retention even important to the mental process? We already talked about shifting your awareness and perspective. We talked about focusing your attention, learning how to think, and understanding how all these things are a journey not a destination. Retaining all this information on your quest to mastering the mind is critical. We retain what we understand; we understand what we pay attention to; and we pay attention to either our desires or what entertains us.

How People Take in Information Determines How They Retain Information.

90% retention if you teach what they learned

75% retention if you practice yourself what you learned

50% retention of what you learned in group discussion

30% retention of what they see demonstrated

20% retention of what they learn visually

10% retention of what they read (unfortunately)

5% retention of what they learn from lectures

How Long They Have This Information Also Dictates Retention

If they have information for 63 days, they retain 17% of that information.

If they have information for 28 days, they retain 19% of that information.

If they have information for 21 days, they retain 18% of that information.

If they have information for 14 days, they retain 21% of that information.

If they have information for 7 days, they retain 35% of that information.

If they have information for 1 day, they retain 54% of that information.

There is no point in learning if you can't retain. Just knowing what retention looks like and where we should focus our energy so that we can get the most out of our learning is important. Here are six keys to retention.

Six Keys to Retention

1) Practice immediately: The faster you put the information to use the more you retain.

2) Don't Ignore What Matters: When you know something is important, you focus, so take notes and give it your full attention.

3) Use Frameworks: Frameworks simplify the message and allow for easier retention, which allows for easier implementation.

4) Use Parables: Connect what you learn to what you already know. This was something that was used by Jesus in the Bible to get people to better understand what was being said so they could live it out.

5) Visualize in Pictures: There is a section in the brain that controls memory, and it operates in pictures. Use this skill for retention.

6) Repeat Often: When trying to retain, constant repetition helps you not forget. Sometimes that is done by repeating it to yourself; other times it's about teaching it to others.

These five phases of the psychological process are key to mental success because you can be aware of what's happening around you and within you. If you can shift your perspective, if you can focus your attention and learn to think and retain, then you can start the process of mastering the mind. These five phases of the psychological process are really the five phases of thought. Everything begins with thought, and understanding those five phases will allow you to ask better questions. Let's go back to the Mental Matrix.

MENTAL MATRIX

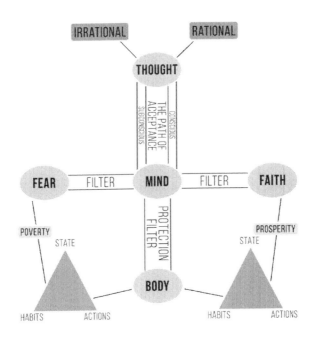

We spoke in the previous chapter about the quality of your questions impacting the quality of your thinking. These questions will allow you to activate your conscious mind, forcing you to think with logic and reason. If you haven't trained your mind and learned how to think like we talked about earlier, then you are putting your success in danger. Here is why it's human nature for the mind to protect the body: If you allow the untrained mind to ask all the questions, then the untrained mind will use the subconscious to answer those questions in ways that will keep you safe.

The problem with that is, safe to my mind means things I know or have experienced or felt. How can you grow to become more when your mind will only direct you to the past that is known, as opposed to the future that is unknown? Success lives outside of your comfort zone, so subconsciously, if your mind is untrained, it will never stretch your comfort zone to reach the success that is outside of it. That is because everything outside of the comfort zone is the land of the unknown. The mind starts asking questions like, "What happens if I do venture out of the comfort zone? What if I get hurt? What if I lose my job? What if I lose my friends? What if I lose my reputation?" There are too many "what ifs" in the mind when it comes to your comfort zone. The untrained subconscious mind says we will not go out there because it is not safe. Your subconscious mind is protecting you, but it is also holding you back from having more success.

Most people live their life never moving forward and not knowing why. They know they want to achieve more, but they are wondering why it's not happening for them, why they can't get themselves to take the proper action, and it's all because their subconscious mind is trying to protect them from harm. Before you get too mad at your subconscious mind, understand this: Everything that your subconscious mind does to protect you does not always hold you back. As a matter a fact, a lot of what your subconscious does keeps you alive and breathing. Imagine if you had to remember to breathe every second—some of you wouldn't be here. Have you ever sat with someone, where you both had a glass of water, and you took a sip, and then the other person took a sip, or vice versa?

This is your subconscious mind serving you. It observed the person drinking and said, that's a good idea, let's drink.

If only it did the same when it came to success. It doesn't naturally serve success because of the nature of uncertainty that comes with success. I do have good news, which is that you can train your subconscious mind to serve you. The way to train the subconscious mind is by the creation of habits that operate on your behalf without your conscious mind. When certain situations happen, you can program your subconscious mind to do what you programmed it to do. Your mind is like a computer—it can only change the operations it was designed to do if programmed to do something different. How do you program your brain? Let's say you have a habit of leaving the toilet seat up. Most don't realize this, and the guys will love me for this and woman not so much. Our subconscious mind believes in the concept of preserving energy as a form of protection. Any energy the mind can save, it will if the task is not important to the mind. The subconscious mind tells the body to leave the toilet seat up to save the useless energy of putting it down because, to most guys, this is not an important action.

All of this is happening in his head without him even knowing it. Ladies, that is why he keeps the toilet seat up, BUT—and that's a big but—here is where I redeem myself with the ladies. You can program your mind to do this by consciously saying to yourself that the act of putting the toilet seat down is an important act. The mind takes the millions of pieces of data it has to sort through constantly and chooses which data is needed and which is not. To do this, the brain creates file drawers in the mind that are important, dangerous, and so on and so forth. This process can be consciously affected if you use your conscious mind to tell your subconscious mind to file putting the toilet seat down in your mind. Every time you go into the bathroom, you have to consciously be aware that you need to put the toilet seat down. You will have to consciously do it a few times, and soon your subconscious mind will kick in and turn it into a habit because your conscious mind told it to.

There are four things that you need to do to create a habit consciously. The habit I created when I stopped cursing was the process, but now I want to show you the practicality of getting it done. By the way, there are really five things, but I talked about the fifth thing already, which is the five phases of the psychological process. You must be able to be aware, have proper perspective and focused attention, and learn to think and retain before you can start to shift a habit, but once you have that down, you can do these four things. Also I should make this note: A change of habit doesn't happen unless you are fully committed to making the change. Just like you can't be half-pregnant, you can't be halfway committed to changing a habit.

Four Ways to Shift a Habit

Trigger

You need something to trigger your mind to be conscious in the time of the action. This has to be something you don't normally do. For example, let's say you want to build the toilet-seat habit.

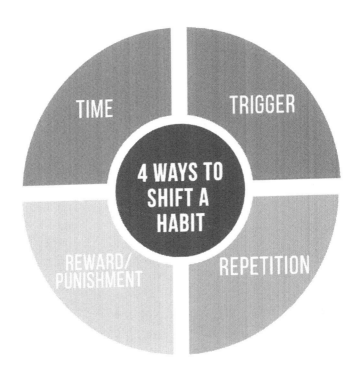

A trigger would be singing a song to yourself every time you have to go to the bathroom. "The toilet seat song, the toilet seat song. Every time I pee and leave the toilet seat up, I am completely wrong!" That song is horrible, but it immediately shifts your state. Let's say you sing that song to yourself every time you go to the bathroom, and that becomes your trigger not to be wrong and to put the toilet seat down. It gets you consciously thinking because it's silly and out of the ordinary, and will remind you to be conscious in the bathroom.

Repetition

You must understand that this habit won't change overnight, and you have to constantly reprogram the mind because the mind will want to go back to what's comfortable. You have to almost whip the mind into submission and turn what was once uncomfortable into something comfortable. The only way to do this is through repetition. When a basketball player wants to learn how to use his left hand more efficiently, the beginning of the battle starts in his mind. His mind is telling him that using this hand is uncomfortable, but if the player is relentless and continues to practice, soon using his left hand is as natural as using his right. That's the power of repetition.

Reward and Punishment

Now punishment doesn't have to be as severe as it sounds. When I was trying to break the habit of cursing, I had a rubber band I put on my wrist and popped myself when I cursed because I wanted to make the change. It was a small punishment, but it was enough of a punishment to get me to literally snap out of it. Your punishment can be as simple as, every time you leave the toilet seat up, you have to sing "I'm a Little Teapot." I don't know why I am obsessed with you singing. A punishment is just there to serve as a reminder (that you don't enjoy) to yourself not to do what you are doing. A reward is for you to celebrate the wins, and that doesn't just mean the large wins. You have to learn to celebrate the small wins as well. Every goal should be broken into milestones, and those milestones should be celebrated. A reward can be giving yourself a pat on the back, a night out with your loved one, or maybe a slice of your favorite cake. Now if you are trying to lose weight, the cake reward should be well prepared in your diet plan because you don't want to create a new habit that you don't want. The purpose of the reward/punishment is to keep you consciously thinking about it.

Time

Nothing can replace time. It took you time to build the habit, and it will take you time to remove it.

In the beginning, you might still be doing the habit you are trying to get rid of, but then you start doing it less and less over time until you stop for good. The reason you have stopped for good is because your subconscious mind took over to create this new habit.

Now I should say, there is one place that the waiting over time to break habits doesn't work, and that's with destructive habits. Habits like drinking, smoking, or doing drugs are habits that could affect your life or the life of someone else. Addictions like this are habits that you can't wean your way off of. You must go full cold-turkey for this, and in this scenario, all the things above still apply, but the one huge layer I would add for this type of habit is accountability. I would say, never attempt to break a destructive habit alone. This is the reason why rehab programs like AA exist. Now if you have a habit that is not a destructive habit but still want to go cold turkey, then you can add that last layer and you are good to go.

This concept of being able to shift habits can change your life if you implement it. Just learning this one process is well worth the cost of the book. I would have loved to understand this early on in my journey to success because I had some horrible habits I needed to change. I want to give you everything I can in this book, but if you were to walk away with just one thing, I think it would make a major impact in your life. Imagine if you could shift any negative habit you ever had to a positive one. You wouldn't even be consciously thinking about the change, but subconsciously you would take the proper action, get the proper results, and get that lifestyle of abundance and prosperity. This process can absolutely get you to the success you desire.

Chapter 4

Development:
The Metamorphosis Process

If the enemy within cannot kill us,
then the enemy without
can do us no harm.

Now that you have an understanding of how you can start the process of mastering your thoughts through the psychological process, you can start the development process that I call the metamorphosis process. The definition of metamorphosis is "the process of transformation from an immature form to an adult form, a change of the form or nature of a thing or person into a completely different thing." I love that definition because of the concept of change of the form into a completely different form. This is what I went through as an 18-year-old kid with very slim chances of succeeding to being where I am today. Every person who has ever had success has been down the path of mental metamorphosis.

What I love about today is that you can go back and see the early days of a person's journey because everything is recorded these days. Imagine if you could go back and hear what the 24-year-old Steve Jobs was thinking while building Apple or if you could see the early days of Phil Knight before he built Nike. The knowledge people would gain when they see what it really takes to win on a high level would be massive. The growth and maturity that you would see from some of the highest achievers in the world would give you hope. People are so busy comparing the person they are today to the greats after they have ascended to greatness. At one point, they didn't know what they were doing, continued to fail, and didn't know how they were ever going to get over the hump. Today you see a great champion, but you missed when they were just amateurs hoping to make their way. Everyone starts as an amateur, and then over time with growth and practice, they become better—and then the best. Realize that this growth is a process, and it doesn't happen overnight.

When I used to coach people, I would ask them to tell me about one of their hobbies they were great at, whether it was sports, painting, singing, or knitting. If it were painting, for example, I asked them to describe their first painting, and they would usually say that it was horrible, that they would throw it in the trash, or that it just looked bad. I would then tell them to look at that first picture and the last picture they painted, and tell me how they compared. They normally said their last picture was great and looked amazing, and everyone wanted it. The biggest difference is time, growth, and practice. In order to become better, you must allow the metamorphosis process to take place.

The beginning of mental development starts with you taking responsibility for you. No one can grow to who they should become until they admit that they were the thing holding themselves back this whole time. I usually ask a person to give me five reasons they feel they aren't where they want to be, and without fail, they can come up with five reasons fairly quickly. Then I tell them something I learned from one of my mentors, Jim Rohn. I tell them there is one problem: You aren't on this list. Where you are today in its totality is 100 percent based on the person you've become up until this point. If you become more, you can have more. It is a constant mental battle to go from where you are now to where you want to be, to go from that immature form to that adult form, but mental development and growth will allow you to start to win that battle.

Most people like to blame their current situation on the things they have gone through in the past. It's not the trials, tribulations, or circumstances that have brought you to where you are now. You are where you are because you thought your way there. When you focus on developing the mental and doing the internal work, the external work becomes easy. The old proverb says, "If the enemy within cannot kill us, then the enemy without can do us no harm." The great thing about the mental metamorphosis is, the more you grow the more inspired and motivated you get because you start to see and feel yourself changing inside. You start to watch yourself respond instead of react, and you see yourself being more positive and focused. Once you start to see that progress, it becomes addictive, and you want to keep growing and keep winning.

I usually tell people it's the first 52 weeks that make all the difference because once you have about one full year of growth under your belt, it's almost impossible to go back to the you that you were before the metamorphosis process. Your mind is like underwear—once it expands, it can never go back to its original state. There are a few great things that will happen for you while you are in the metamorphosis process:

WHERE YOU ARE TODAY IN ITS TOTALITY IS 100% BASED ON THE PERSON YOU BECOME UP UNTIL THIS POINT

#TheMentalPlaybook
#MentalAsset

I usually tell people it's the first 52 weeks that make all the difference because once you have about one full year of growth under your belt, it's almost impossible to go back to the you that you were before the metamorphosis process. Your mind is like underwear—once it expands, it can never go back to its original state. There are a few great things that will happen for you while you are in the metamorphosis process:

- You will start to get clarity on your purpose.
- You will be inspired to set, plan, and achieve your goals.
- You will start to develop effective schedule-management skills for optimal effectiveness and achievement.
- You will begin to handle problems like a pro, never letting any problems rock your boat.
- You will start to become a better leader, mastering the art of relationship building.
- You will develop greater resilience than others because of your commitment to be better.
- You will become more valuable to the world than you ever dreamed possible.

As you develop in the mental metamorphosis process, there are a few things you need to beware of that can stop your growth in its tracks. These five things have taken some of the highest achievers and brought them back to down to reality. You don't want to get caught up in any of these because they can block you from success. I call them the Five Mental Traps.

Five Mental Traps

Ego:

As you grow, you might notice yourself be-coming the person people find themselves going to when they have problems. It's easy to get a big head when you feel like you have the answers. You want to beware of becoming an egomaniac. We used to say all the time that E.G.O. is Edging God Out. Don't allow your ego to take you out like too many past successful people. Mike Tyson was the baddest man to step into the boxing ring. People would literally fly from around the world and pay tens of thousands of dollars to watch him box even knowing that most of his bouts rarely ever got out of the first round. Professional boxers who made their living going to battle in the ring were genuinely afraid of him, and he knew it. His ego got to him, and he let the praise and money get to his head. He stopped training as hard because he thought he was the greatest that the world had ever seen. Because of this attitude, he ended up going into a title fight with Buster Douglas while out of shape and unfocused. Buster Douglas shocked the world when he knocked out Mike Tyson, and that was the beginning of the decline of the great Iron Mike Tyson. His career ended sooner because of ego. Always remember that you are never as good as they say you are, and you are never as bad as they say you are.

Don't Stop Growing:

The three most common words in mediocrity are "I know that." We have never reached a celling of information, and we are never done growing and becoming better. Those who understand what it takes to succeed continue to buy books, continue to go to the seminars, and continue to hire the best trainers because they understand the value of being a continual learner. When you step into my car, 90 percent of the time, you will hear people like Les Brown, Tony Robbins, or Brian Tracy. Every day, I am committed to learning ways to be a better Eugene than I was yesterday.

Treating Others Horribly:

While you are growing and achieving, you must realize that no matter how much success you might have, being knowledgeable, successful, or famous does not place you on a pedestal of importance. This is why I love the story of Jesus, and if you ever want to get a guide on leadership, go read the four books of the Gospels Matthew, Mark, Luke, and John. Jesus is supposed to be the person with all the power and all the fame, the man who healed and fed thousands. After a meal, there was a tradition in the culture in those days to wash your feet before you walked through the house because they didn't want to track dust all around the house. Jesus, being the leader, decided to wash his people's feet, and none of them understood why he of all people would do this, and I love what he said. He said, "You do not realize now what I am doing, but later you will understand ... You call me 'Teacher' and 'Lord,' and rightly so, for that is what I am. Now that I, your Lord and Teacher, have washed your feet, you also should wash one another's feet. I have set you an example that you should do as I have done for you. I tell you the truth, no servant is greater than his master, nor is a messenger greater than the one who sent him. Now that you know these things, you will be blessed if you do them." (John 13:7 and 13–17) These wise words show the level of humility that he had even being who he was in that community. My thought is, if Jesus didn't feel like he was better than anyone, you shouldn't either.

Never Forget Where You Came From:

It's said that the minute you forget where you came from, you are on your way back there, and I believe it. Sometimes in the growth of becoming this new person, we forget about the old person we were. Now I'm not saying you should be that old person, but I am saying that you should remember the journey that brought you to where you are. Remember the lessons, struggles, and triumphs as you grow to the next phase in your life because being that person you want to be means not just learning in the moment but also getting on-the-job training. Use your past as a guide to help you get past things that once held you up.

Never Forget Your Mission and Vision:

Having success, making money, traveling the world, and being famous is fine, but the truly great understand it's about more than having stuff. The greats know that true success and fulfillment comes from making an impact that is greater than yourself. We discussed earlier that the two things that bring joy are growing and giving. There is something that keeps the motivation high when you are fighting for something bigger. This also means not allowing people to speak against your mission or vision. My favorite line is, let no man steal your vision because no man gave it to you. The reason I love that quote so much and have it on my office wall is because I believe that people let the negative words of family, friends, and neighbors knock them off the path of their mission and vision. Losing your focus on your mission is a pitfall you want to avoid.

It's important that I give you these things as a reminder that when you are on this growth journey to go from one form to the next, it is easy to lose track of who you need to become and who you don't need to become. While people are in the metamorphosis process, they start looking around at other people in their own process and try to do one of two things, either compare themselves or copy the other person's process. In Silicon Valley during the height of Steve Job's

Apple run, people felt the need to try to be like Steve and be a dictator-type CEO who yells at his people. A lot of people failed trying to be something they weren't. Be aware of these five things. Be aware of why you are in this process of growth in the first place.

When I think about the metamorphosis process, I think about baby kittens because before we succeed, we are all little baby kittens with lions inside of us. Every day with every goal and every dream, this lion is crying to get out. You know this because every person on the planet has a desire to be more, have more, or do more. Most people suppress that desire out of fear, and they don't try to move forward because even if they don't move forward, at least they won't move backward. The problem with that philosophy is that there is no such thing as neutrality. By the law of nature, you are either moving forward or moving backward. There is no such thing as standing still. Nothing ever stays the way it is, and trying to keep it that way is ignorant.

The law of laws is cause and effect—what you sow you shall reap, and what you reap you shall sow. As you learn and grow through your metamorphosis process, you will learn not just to know these laws but to live by them. Like I said earlier, the most exciting thing is seeing yourself grow and become better. I remember that when I got into that first business at 18 years old, in order for me to get clients, I had to go prospecting, meaning I had to go meet and talk to new people. That was a foreign thing to me at the time because I was an introvert. Now no one ever believes that I was once an introvert, but I was. I never was a big talker. I never tried to be the life of the party. I always kept to myself and liked it that way. Even my wife would tell you, I can be alone and quiet for long periods of time. I have trained myself to be an extrovert because I had to in order to be good at business.

Talking to complete strangers was totally outside of my comfort zone. Not only that, but I just wasn't good at it because I wasn't confident. I didn't know what to say, and when I got nervous, I stuttered. I had a goal to grow this business and get better, so I talked to hundreds of random people on the streets over the course of six weeks. The first week, I talked to a little over 200 people, and I was horrible. Every person I talked to said no, but at the end of that first week, I was no longer as afraid as I was before. The next week, I talked to about 150 people, and I had an idea how to approach people in an unthreatening way. In week three, I started to figure out what to say and what not to say. By week four, my confidence had peaked, and I really was starting to feel comfortable in my own skin. By week five, I felt like a juggernaut. I had my lines to say; my smile was ready; and I knew how to approach people. People felt comfortable giving me their contact info for a follow-up call. Finally, week six, I gave it my all, felt like a pro, and was having a good time. Over those six weeks, I talked to just under 1,000 people, and in that time, I understood how to talk to any person at any time for anything. It was one of the best growth experiences I have ever been through. Now I know what some of you are thinking: He must have sold the product to dozens and dozens of people. But the truth is, out of all those people, I got about 10 people interested and only signed up one person. Most people would say that was a waste of time, but I say that was one of the most valuable times of my life. It broke me so far out of my comfort zone and helped me become someone I never thought I would become. It was like I put myself through a solo boot-camp with me, myself, and I. Imagine the mental fortitude a person needs to have in order to get hundreds and hundreds of no's and not lose their excitement and energy. These types of growth moments happen in the metamorphosis process.

Okay, so how does all of this connect to the Mental Matrix?

MENTAL MATRIX

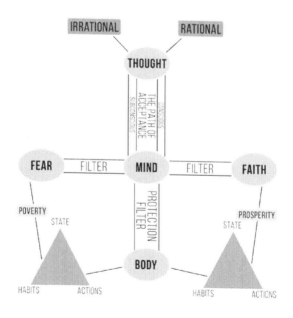

The central point of the metamorphosis process is the mind, and we said that the questions you ask and the answers you give affect your thoughts, and your thoughts are transferred to your mind through what I call the path of acceptance. Any time a thought enters your mind, whether it's through your conscious or subconscious, it must accept that thought as truth or reject that thought as false. This is why development of the mind is so important because the more you develop your mind the more you strengthen the path of acceptance to serve your success instead of creating your failure. What do I mean by all of this? I mean that every thought is analyzed by the conscious or subconscious and then filtered to faith or to fear.

Let me give you an example. Let's say you think a thought like, "I am too fat to run a marathon." That thought begins to travel down the path of acceptance and is answered by either your conscious or subconscious mind. Let's say your subconscious mind answers that question and says, "Yup, you are too fat to run a marathon. What are you thinking? You just ate a whole large pizza by yourself. You never run marathons. It is impossible!" That thought is now accepted as truth and filtered to fear, and the fear causes you to be in a negative state and take no action, and the building blocks of your habits lead you to poverty. This is the first path of the Four Mental Pathways. The first path is Thought > Subconscious > Fear > Poverty.

Now let's say your conscious answers the question this time. When the thought goes to your conscious, remember we said it goes to a rational thought process. It takes the statement, "I am too fat to run a marathon," and rationally thinks through it. It travels through the path of acceptance and accepts it as truth. Let's say you have tried to run a marathon before and failed, or your mother, father, sister, or brother said you were too fat, and you believed them. At this point, your conscious sends that thought to fear, which leads to a negative state, no action, and building the foundational blocks of bad habit. This is the second path of the Four Mental Pathways. The second path is Thought > Conscious > Fear > Poverty.

Now let's say your conscious answers this time, and because you have been going through the metamorphosis process, your mind rationally thinks about that statement through a new perspective. Since you have been growing and developing, your mind searches the new programming you did mentally and finds a quote from a book you read that said, "Impossible is a word to be found only in a dictionary of fools," and you're no fool, so your conscious mind rejects the statement, which leads to a positive state, creates positive actions, and begins building the foundational blocks of positive habit. This is the third path of the Four Mental Pathways. The third path is Thought > Conscious > Faith > Prosperity.

The last pathway is the most important one when it comes to achieving at the highest levels. Before I explain this, I should say that no one is exempt from stupid thoughts that travel to the mind every once in a while. The people who achieve at the highest levels hear the statement, "I am too fat to run a marathon," and because they have dedicated themselves to the metamorphosis process, they have trained their mind to immediately take a negative thought and reject it subconsciously. The mind doesn't need to pull quotes from a book to reject the statement, but it might pull from experiences as an achiever to reinforce that belief. This is the fourth path of the Four Mental Pathways.

The fourth path is Thought > Subconscious > Faith > Prosperity. This fourth pathway is the ultimate way to think for high achievers, but to be clear, even the highest achievers don't operate in this fourth path all the time. They do operate in this pathway 70 to 80 percent of the time.

When your mind is operating in the fourth path, your subconscious is rejecting thoughts as false, and that leads to a positive state, which creates positive actions and a house of habits. The reason I call it a house of habits is because you need to operate in pathway three over and over again so that pathway four becomes as natural and automatic as breathing. These habits lead to prosperity. Always remember that your mind will accept what you allow it to accept because you are in control.

You have heard me refer to fear and faith, so why do I call it fear and faith? It's because I believe that every thought accepted or rejected in the mind and causing the body to feel, think, and act in a certain way always leads to fear or faith. I believe that fear and faith are the primary drivers in the human experience. The definition of fear is "an unpleasant emotion caused by the belief that someone or something is dangerous, likely to cause pain or is a threat." Remember what I said earlier: The mind is designed to protect the body at all times. This is why it's impossible for you to hold on to your own nose and suffocate yourself. Your mind will go into protection mode and force you to pass out so that it can take full control of your breathing again. Fear is not always negative; it can keep you aware of danger, like getting hit by a car or falling items. Here is the problem with the mind that produces fear: It does not understand success and failure. It only speaks the language of protection.

When you tell your body to do something that creates fear, your mind can't function. Here is the thing: Human beings have the ability to adapt. Adaption is very effective but takes repetition and time to master. For example, when we travel to high-altitude areas, our bodies adjust so that our cells still receive sufficient oxygen. In high-altitude places, your body will adjust slowly, but the more times you go to high-altitude places and the longer you stay the better the body will adjust. It's the same in your mind.

FEAR AND FAITH ARE THE PRIMARY DRIVERS IN THE HUMAN EXPERIENCE

#TheMentalPlaybook
#MentalAsset

Your mind is in a constant state of keeping you sane and functioning. You can adapt your mind by feeding it new information in the metamorphosis process. The more you feed it with new information and the longer you spend processing that information the more your subconscious can start to take over the process for you.

Now your mind is not only trying to protect you but also trying to propel you because creating success is another form of protection if you build your mind to see it that way. I used to believe it was all about eliminating fear, but it's about reprogramming fear to see not succeeding as harmful to the mind and body.

How do you do this? You will never get away from fear, but you can use the natural responses to fear along with the metamorphosis process to develop ways to trick the mind into thinking that going after this success is actually protecting you.

Five Steps to Reprogram Fear into Faith

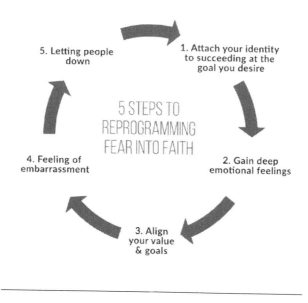

Step 1: *Attach Your Identity to Succeeding at the Goal You Desire*

The mind doesn't want to operate in anything that is incongruent to how it sees itself. If you attach your identity to the success, not having that success means you are out of alignment with who you have told yourself you need to be. Your mind will fight to align itself with who you believe you should be versus who you actually are. The key to this is truly identifying yourself with the goal you desire. You can't kind of believe you are the goal; you have to truly believe not having the goal makes you less you. That feeling drives the mind to adjust and make it a reality. A great way to do this is affirmations. This is why effective affirmations start with "I am": "I am fit," or "I am a millionaire." Someone once said to me, if you tell yourself something you aren't, then you are lying to yourself. What I believe is that you are telling the truth in advance. One caveat is that you must truly attach yourself to the goal and identify with it because if you don't, then your mind won't try to align with the goal, which means your mind won't take the actions necessary. With no actions, affirmations are just wishes.

Step 2: *Gain Deep Emotional Feelings*

The book *Think and Grow Rich* by Napoleon Hill calls this idea "burning desire." Once again, if you connect emotionally to the goals, your mind feels the hurt and pain of not having it. Remember, fear is about the belief of present pain, and if you emotionally feel hurt about not having your goals, then your mind will work harder toward changing that fact to get out of pain.

Step 3: *Align Your Value and Goals*

So many people say they want to make more money, but their value systems believe that people with money are bad people. These incongruences don't allow for them to make money. Flipping it to allow fear to work for you would be saying, "My value system is that I always had money, so not having money is hurtful to me." If you can get your values and goals aligned, then the fear of not being aligned will get your mind to create what you want. Have you ever had a number in your mind of an amount of money you need to always see in your bank account for you to feel comfortable? Like if you had less than $500 in the bank, you would start to panic? This means the value and goals you have are standardized at $500. Your mind and body will find ways to stay at that number. Your mind and body would do the same thing at $1,000, $10,000, $100,000, and $1 million. Your mind must always align with your values.

Step 4: *The Feeling of Embarrassment*

As much as we don't like to admit it, we care what other people think about us. Even if we say we don't care, we should care a little bit. Why not use this to your benefit? Put yourself out there by being bold enough to declare your goals to people you respect and care about who can, with respect, hold you accountable. Putting yourself out there forces you to take the necessary actions because the mind wants to avoid the pain of people laughing at you or talking about you in a negative light. That feeling of embarrassment will trigger the mind to align with the goals.

Step 5: *Letting People Down*

Even stronger than the desire to protect yourself is the desire to protect those you love and care about. Having something that you are fighting for that is bigger than yourself will always drive you because of the fear of letting down people you care about.

I have told you about why I refer to it as fear on one side, and now I'll talk about why I refer to it as faith on the other side. Remember, I said that I believe every thought that is accepted or rejected in the mind and causes the body to feel, think, and act in a certain way always leads to fear or faith. I believe that fear and faith are the primary drivers in the human experience. The definition of faith is "complete trust or confidence in someone or something, certainty." It is difficult for the mind to act in faith because faith is trust and certainty for things that haven't happened yet, and when you think rationally, it is easy to dismiss the things you don't see and accept only the things you see. One of the reasons that is difficult is because most people try to have faith in too many things.

They have faith in the person who will never hurt them in a relationship; they have faith in the diet; they have faith that the check will come in the mail; they have faith that the kids will be good in school; they have faith that the car won't crash; and they have faith that when they sit in a chair, the chair will hold. If you look at life, there are a million things to have faith in. Let me ask you a question: Is it possible that the person does hurt you? Is it possible the diet doesn't work? Is it possible the check won't come in the mail? The answer is yes, of course, so if you put your faith in all these things and a large majority of them don't work out, then how do you feel about this faith thing? No wonder people lack faith.

With all of this, I believe most people look at faith the wrong way. I believe people should stop having faith in everything and only have faith in two things. The first one is optional, but I am a man of faith, so I say put your faith in God, the one person who can't fail you. The second thing is having faith that no matter what happens, everything will always work itself out. The good book says you can have the faith of a grain of mustard seed—not faith like a mountain, just a mustard seed.

Do you know how small a mustard seed is? All you need to focus on is that it all will work itself out. If you have that philosophy, then you always have the fortitude to move forward. Nothing can stop my progress because I don't need anything to happen for me to feel accomplished. All I have to do is one thing: move forward. If more people took on this philosophy, not only would they be able to endure faith longer but they would be able to overcome obstacles set before them on their path of success. How do you have this level of faith?

Faith always seems like this esoteric thing that is unable to be attained, but the truth is that faith is as practical as going to the bathroom. There are six cornerstone things you must do to build and grow your faith.

Six Cornerstones of Faith

6 CORNERSTONES OF FAITH

BE PATIENT

EXPECTATION

FEED YOUR FAITH

PROTECT YOUR FAITH

GET AROUND YOUR FAITH

ACT OF YOUR FAITH

1) Be Patient: Everyone wants things to happen quickly; they want it now. Most people's faith only lasts a short time because if they don't see it quickly enough, they don't want to have faith. One of my favorite quotes is, "Success is merely holding on

when others have just let go." Having faith doesn't mean you are problem-free. It means when the problems come, you will be focused. Patience allows you to wait out the storm. The more patient you are the more things come to you. Rushing is a sign of desperation, and desperation is a repellent of people, opportunities, and success. This doesn't mean you must move slowly, but you must understand that success is never on your time schedule. You usually never see the finish line from the beginning, but having faith is knowing the line is there, and having patience is being willing to go on the journey to that finish line.

2) Expectation: It is hard to have faith when you expect negativity and hardship. Expectation is the breeding ground of miracles. Faith and expectation are one. Expectation is really about what you see. If what you see currently is now what you saw, then what you see is temporary, and most people trust their sight more than their vision. I have always believed that the eyes have stolen more dreams than the hands. It's not that most people can't do it; it's

that they don't expect to succeed doing it, and that lack of expectation is lack of faith. We can create our own heartbreak or happiness through expectation. When our expectation of outcomes are high, our belief is high.

3) Feed Your Faith: If you want your faith to grow, you must feed it. Faith is like a baby in the beginning. You feed it baby food and then regular food. What do you feed your faith?

   A) Philosophies of Success

   B) Words of Affirmations

   C) Positive Thoughts

   Your faith must eat, and it's your job to feed it. If you don't feed the baby, what happens? Most people have been bad parents to their faith because their faith is dead due to neglect. And just like if you neglect to feed a baby and the baby dies, you go to jail, if you neglect to feed your faith, then your success goes to jail.

4) Protect Your Faith: Life is always about building and protecting. When you want to get your body

right, you work out (building) and you eat right (protecting). When you want to get your finances right, you make more (building) and you save more (protecting). Not only do you build your faith but you must protect it from the outside voices that want to steal your value. They say the biggest killer of success is your friends, family, and neighbors. You need to protect your faith constantly. My quote I say all the time is, "Let no man steal your vision because no man gave it to you." This statement is a statement of protection. Your faith can be stolen if you allow it, so protect it.

5) Get Around Faith: This is how you stop faith from being stolen. Surround yourself with people of faith. Your environment can make or break you if you allow it. I remember going to the Tony Robbins event where he had people walk on fire with fire coals over 1,000 degrees. I was a bit nervous, but because there were so many people who had faith and walked across the coals, the environment gave me faith to do it myself. Phycology would call

it social pressure. I encourage you to get some positive social pressure in your life. You can usually tell how much success a person has by the company they keep.

6) Acts of Faith: If you have even a small bit of faith, act on it. If you act on faith, you get more experience. That experience builds confidence, and that creates more faith. The distance between the thing you have faith in and that thing being a reality is called action. Actions are the fundamental key to increasing your faith.

This explains both sides of fear and faith. Every thought that is accepted or rejected in the mind and causes the body to feel, think, and act in a certain way always leads to fear or faith. Fear and faith are the primary drivers in the human experience.

THE BIGGEST KILLER OF SUCCESS IS YOUR FRIENDS, FAMILY AND NEIGHBORS

#TheMentalPlaybook
#MentalAsset

Chapter 5

Habit:
The Behavioral Process

*Without permanent
habits, you can't create
consistent success.*

As a leader, I have had the opportunity to lead many great people, from college students all the way up to doctors, CEOs, and lawyers. The majority of these relationships were amazing and fruitful, but there was one frustrating individual named Tim (not his real name). No matter what I did for Tim or what I said to him, he would agree and want to make the change but would never do the things he knew he needed to do to be successful. I tried for months and months to get him to shift his behavior to create habits that would serve him. It never worked until I realized one thing that I never noticed before. The whole time, I had been trying to get Tim to change his behavior, but not once did I try to find out why he had the behavior he had and what parts of his thinking created that behavior in the first place. I had to learn that every behavior starts in the mind.

This is why the Mental Matrix starts with thoughts, because if you have not correctly changed your psychological process and grown your mentality with the metamorphosis process, then your behavior won't change and you will keep making the same mistakes, doing the same things over and over.

If our behavior is not serving us, we need to make some assessments. What behaviors are you doing? Are those behaviors serving your success, and how do you make those changes? There are three major ways you can assess your behavior. For those who are self-aware, this can be a simple process, but for those who are not self-aware, you might have been stuck trying to get clarity on your behavior and how it impacts your results.

<u>Three Ways to Assess Behavior</u>

1. Introspection

You must learn to look within and not without. This is a trap many people fall into because they are so focused on blaming that they haven't taken time to look at what behaviors they have that take them farther away from their goals. Most people look at this as a hard thing, but it's really not. If you just take the time to sit down in silence with yourself, you could learn a lot. Here is my suggestion of what I believe you should do to have moments of introspection.

This process is simple:

A) Sit alone in a room with no distraction.

B) Have a list of questions for yourself about what behavior you want to analyze.

Example: How do I feel when I do this behavior?

What am I thinking about during these times?

How do I react when this happens to me?

C) Take the time to write down the answers.

If you take the time to do this, you will have a clear sense of how you feel, see things, and react by looking within, but the key to this is not lying to yourself.

2. **Observation**

Either currently or in the past, try to observe what you do, how you feel, and what you say when certain things happen. Sometimes you need others who are willing to be observers for you to help you see the things you can't. Also keep in mind that there is a chance the observer, whether you or an outside person, will give a subjective or prejudiced report. Looking directly at situations can allow you to assess what behaviors you take in certain instances.

3. Survey

Another way you can assess your behavior is by surveying. This is when you survey the closest people to you and ask for their opinion. If you do this, you must make them feel safe to tell the truth without losing the relationship. The rule is, when they are answering your questions, you are not allowed to defend yourself—only take notes and be extremely grateful that you have good friends who will tell you the truth. After assessing yourself, you may see some things you like and maybe others you don't like. The age-old question is, "Why do I do what I do?"

These three things allow you to assess where your behaviors are, because if you don't even know what you are doing that's holding you back, how can you make the change. Now before I talk about how this ties in to the Mental Matrix, I want to talk about the influences of your behavior. There are six things that influence a person's behavior; these six things tend to create the habits, which create the actions, which create a life of prosperity or poverty.

Six Behavioral Influences

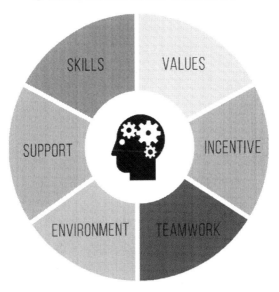

Six Behavioral Influences

1. Values

All consistent actions taken by an individual must align with their values if they are to feel happy. People cannot operate successfully if they are incongruent to their values. This is why some people commit suicide, because they feel like their life today does not add up to the value that they feel it should. Rather than living with that value imbalance, they would rather not live. It might be time to assess your value and see what values you hold. Are they what you want? Do they serve you? Are your values outdated? Are they carrying someone else's values? Like a company, the values they hold will not only determine what people do and don't do but they will determine the type of people who come into the organization. Like a company, you need to sit down and assess your values. Get clear on the values you want that will serve you moving forward because your values have a large impact on your behavior.

2. Skills

Contrary to popular belief, a person's resistance to change does not always stem from a lack of motivation, but rather their opposition to change is often produced by their lack of skills. This one is not clear at first glance, but if you don't have the ability to do a thing, then there is a likely chance that you won't do it. I truly believe that a person's skills absolutely affect their behavior. Understanding what to do, how to do it, and what tactics are needed, and having confidence in those abilities helps you not to quit. If you really think about it, successful skills can be the all-time great driver of behavior.

Think about a kid who loves to talk and debate, and then the parent reinforces that by saying, "Yes, this kid is the greatest debater." Because the kid debates well and has the feeling of accomplishment, that kid will do it again and again. The cycle continues until the skills get so great and the kid is so competent that their behavior continues in the same direction subconsciously. No one likes to be bad at anything. If you lack natural skills and you don't have the ability, then you will want to do it. You will try and not be successful, and then you will not do it again. Whether or not you have the skills in a thing determines your behavior.

3. Teamwork

In teamwork, the sum is greater than its parts. Humans are naturally pack animals, and we would rather be in a group than be alone even if it's one person. There was a study done in a hospital waiting room where they tested whether people would take an action if those around them took action. There were three people who sat in a waiting room and were all in the know about this study. Then they introduced a new woman who knew nothing about what was going on. When a bell rang, the three people who knew all stood up at the sound and sat right back down. The one who didn't know wondered why they stood up but made no reaction. Then the bell rang again, and the three stood up but the girl didn't. Now she was really confused as to why they were standing up every time the bell rang. By the third bell, she reluctantly stood up when everyone stood. By the fourth and fifth time the bell rang, she stood up like nothing was wrong.

Then they added more new people who didn't know about the study, and they had the same reaction as the girl, but over time, they all stood up as well. Then they slowly started to take the original three people out of the room, and like clockwork, all of the new people stood at the bell. People will be influenced to take actions if they are in a group even if they don't understand why they are doing it. Because we would rather work together than alone, we normally would not take major action without a team even if that team is only one or two. Having a team or people with you will dramatically affect what you do or don't do.

4. Support

Our peer groups have an immense influence on our behaviors and decisions. We are strongly influenced by the approval of others, and we can leverage our social support groups to take advantage of what we already know. We must learn to enlist the support of the right people.

5. Incentive

The first thing we think about is changing the person to change the behavior, but sometimes you must change the things around a person to change their behavior. Rewards, bonuses, perks, benefits, and recognition can all be effective motivators to behavior and influence how much or how little a person does. The problem with incentives is that most leaders usually use this as the first way to get a person to change their behavior.

6. Environment

Environment has always and will always influence people. If you are in the environment of rich people, you are likely to get richer. If you are in the environment of poor people, you are likely to get poorer. Athletes are likely to develop athletes; musicians develop musicians; and poets develop poets.

It is sometimes the parent who forces the outcome, but most times, the parent doesn't have to do anything. The environment will make major impacts on the behavior of the person.

With all of that said, how does the behavioral process operate within the Mental Matrix? First let's start with a recap. When you think about the questions you ask and how they determine your thoughts/thinking, your thinking is accepted by your mind and is filtered through fear or faith. The mind and the body are one, and the connection of the mind and body is the protection filter. The mind's number-one job is to protect the body. Any desire to have success or achievement usually happens outside of the comfort zone. Outside of the comfort zone is unknown, so there is no way for the mind to keep you protected in the un-known. The mind's default is to keep you in the com-fort zone to keep you safe. If you allow this process to happen unchecked, you will never achieve at the levels you desire.

The mind gives the body direction and controls three elements of your behavior. I call them the Three Behavioral Triggers:

1. State: emotions, how you feel
2. Actions: things you do, actions you take
3. Habits: things you repeatedly do without con-scious thinking

These three things can be either positive or nega-tive, leading you to poverty or prosperity.

1) State

Your state determines how you feel and the emo-tions you deal with on a day-to-day, minute-by-minute basis. There are four specific things that can affect your state.

Your Physical Body

Your physical body constantly has an impact on the way you feel from day to day. From a health perspective, if you are overweight, you feel differently than if you are in shape. You have more energy and enthusiasm when you attack the day. Also when you look at yourself in the mirror, do you like what you see? Are you comfortable in your own skin? These things affect how you feel every day. Also what you wear has a big impact on how you feel, and that doesn't mean you need expensive clothes. When you put on your best clothes and look your best, you feel your best. The physical body has more of an impact on your state and overall success than most people give it.

Your Attention

What you focus on has an impact on your success. The things you think about, whether positive or negative, impact your state. If you focus your attention on how bad life is, how much you hate your job, and how much debt you are in, you will get more of those things. As humans, we are emotional creatures, and yes, men, you are included in that. As emotional creatures, we normally get emotionally tied in to the problems in our life, and being emotionally tied in to negative situations will make you ultimately negative. Watch what you focus on because where your awareness flows, your energy goes, and you want your energy going to the positive not the negative.

How You Speak

What you say has a huge effect on how you feel. What you say to others shapes what you feel. If you often get into arguments, are rude to people, and walk around angry, then there is a strong likelihood that your state is not in the most joyous place. It's not just how you speak to others; it's how you speak to yourself. I will talk more about this later, but the words you say to yourself have a major impact on the way you feel from day to day.

What Things Mean

The last thing that impacts your state is the meaning you give the things that happen to you in life. When things happen to you, negative or positive, how do you feel about it, and what do you say it means? The same negative thing can happen to two different people, and two different people will have it mean two different things to them. One person loses his leg in the service, and if you ask him how he feels about it, he says, "It was an honor to be in battle for my country, and I don't regret a thing."

If you ask another person the same thing, they may say, "I wish I never would have gone. What am I going to do without a leg? My life is over." Now these are two different people with the same situation, but they assigned two different meanings to them. Which of the two do you think was happy, and which was in borderline depression? This can even happen in positive things. A woman finds $100 on the floor and says, "Of course I find this money. Nothing but good things happen to me all the time." Another woman finds $100 and says, "Man, this is probably the best thing that will happen to me today, and the rest of the day must be destined for bad luck." The way you define the things in your life can force you into a state that you may or may not want.

When it comes to your state, positive thoughts create a positive mindset, and a positive mindset creates a positive state.

2) Actions

When a thought comes in and you have been growing mentally, you make conscious decisions to take an action that will serve your success. All the actions you take run through conscious or subconscious thought, and they are made positive or negative based on your philosophies. All actions lead to an outcome, and that outcome is totally up to you. If you want a prosperous outcome, you make a decision that aligns with your goals, values, and desires. If you want a negative outcome—and I don't know why you would—you make decisions based on an untrained mind that is looking to protect you and keep you safely in your comfort zone.

3) Habits

When the conscious mind is in the correct state and takes the correct philosophies consistently, over time those correct philosophies become correct actions that become habits. Long-lasting habits are normally operating fully from the subconscious mind. Habits are the true way to lifelong success. When you look at some of the highest achievers in the world, you know that they have created some world-class habits. There is one word above all words that drives habits, and that word is *perspective*.

Perspective is driven by your subconscious thinking. My definition of habit is your mental design. In your mind, there is a structured design that triggers actions without any conscious thought. This action causes a result, and everyone is trying to change their results by forcing new actions. Unless the perspective changes, the actions can change temporarily but won't change permanently. Without permanent habits, you can't create consistent success. A lot of a person's perspective comes from the people who raised them. The average person's thoughts are really not their thoughts but the thoughts passed to them by others over time. You must learn to change your mental perspective and get away from habits that don't serve you. There are five days that you must have to break those bad habits.

WITHOUT PERMANENT HABITS YOU CAN'T CREAT CONSISTENT SUCCESS

#TheMentalPlaybook
#MentalAsset

5 DAYS OF
BREAKING A HABIT

DAY OF DISGUST

DAY OF DESIRE

DAY OF DECISION

DAY OF ACTION

DAY OF RESOLVE

5 Days of Breaking Habits

Day 1: The Day of Disgust: This is the day when you say enough is enough, I have had all that I can take. I remember that day for me with my health. In my early years, I was an athlete in good shape, played basketball 10 or 15 times a week, and pretty much ate what I wanted and didn't gain much, but when I moved to California, I no longer played sports as much but kept eating as if I was still as active as when I was in New York. Also, early on, I was broke, so it was rare that I would eat much. I started making some money and eating at nice restaurants. Over time with no workout plan, I started gaining more and more. I knew I had gained weight, but I would not get on the scale because I didn't want to face the reality of what that number was. One day, I decided I would get on the scale, and it said 300 pounds. I was in shock and in tears that I had let it go that far. I said enough was enough. I went on a diet and workout plan, and lost 55 pounds. Even though it has been better, I am still not 100 percent where I want to be, but now I am happier with where I am than where I was before. I am on another 12-month run to drop another 30 pounds to be at the perfect weight for me.

Day 2: The Day of Desire: It wasn't enough for me to be disgusted with where I was. I had to also have enough desire to change. I always wanted to change my body, but sometimes desire waits for a trigger, and that trigger might come from a book (hopefully this book), a seminar, a song, an inspirational video on social media, a conversation with a loved one, an experience, a confrontation with an enemy, or maybe just the bathroom scale, like what happened for me. Anything can trigger a desire when that day of disgust has hit and the desire is triggered, which sometimes happens the same day and sometimes doesn't. When it is triggered, you can go on to the next day.

Day 3: The Day of Decision: Disgust can piss you off, but with time, you could convince yourself to live with the thing you really didn't want and make excuses for why it's not a problem anymore. A day of desire can come to you in a moment of inspiration, but it can fade over time. The day of decision is something different. When you look at the word *decide* and break it down to its suffix and prefix, the word becomes similar to words like *pesticide* (death to bugs), *homicide* (death to others), and *suicide* (death to self). I believe that the word *decide* means death to all other options. It wasn't enough for me to be disgusted with the weight gain, and it wasn't enough for me to desire to take the weight off. I had to decide I was going to do it now.

Day 4: The Day of Action: Just like in the day of decision, all these days can happen in one day or multiple days, but they all hinge on the others. There is something called the law of diminishing intent. If you intend or decide to make a change but it is not followed by actions, then you haven't really made a decision. Remember that consistent actions are driven by your psychological process. Proper thinking will build proper actions, which done consistently, build habits, and habits build consistent actions, which get you consistent positive results. This day of action is key to you living in prosperity instead of poverty.

Day 5: The Day of Resolve: I love what Jim Rohn said. He said that when he was speaking at a kids' school, he asked them what they thought resolve meant, and one of the little girls said, "Resolve is promising yourself you will never give up." Just because you go through these days doesn't mean you don't get discouraged, and it doesn't mean you get off track. In that 12-month process, I had some bad days, but I never let the bad day turn into a bad week or a bad month, or quit altogether. You must hit a point of resolve that says, "I will do it, or I will die." Benjamin Disraeli said, "Nothing will resist the human will that will stake its existence on its purpose." If it's not a real day of disgust, desire, decision, action, and resolve, then your excitement might last for a week, a month, or a quarter, but it won't last for a lifetime.

This is why every step in the Mental Matrix is so important, because each section is a building block over another. If you want massive success, you must create the habits of a high achiever, but you can't do that without the psychological process and the mental metamorphosis process. After you focus on shifting your thinking and growing, you shift your focus to these three triggers. The reason there are only a few people who have success in life is because there are only a few people who even know how to master any of these things we talked about so far. My hope is to demystify the idea of a person who is a high achiever. It's not luck; they don't have the most talent; and they aren't prettier, taller, or anything like that. It's simply because they have decided to master the Mental Matrix.

Whether they call it that or not, every successful person has mastered it. A lot of success is all about seeking out the proper knowledge.

The reason people talk about luck is because they are trying to justify why they aren't in the position to succeed. Most people haven't even tried and can't admit that they are where they are because of the decisions they have made. There is a saying that says we are all self-made but only the successful will admit it. I agree with the premise of that statement, which is really saying the successful know that if they want to succeed, they need to get off their butt and make it happen. Though no one ever got there alone, the attitude of knowing no one is going to do it for you is a necessity.

Have you ever heard the saying that knowledge is power? Also have you heard people's response that no, only applied knowledge is power? Have you ever wondered why applied knowledge is power? It's because knowing something and not doing it is a flaw of the mind. It's the proper thinking that turns desires into dreams realized. One of the problems is figuring out what you want in the first place. One of the first books I ever read fully was *Think and Grow Rich* by Napoleon

Hill, and one of the principles in the book is being crystal clear about what you want. I encourage you to take a second and write down one to three goals you can achieve this year that will help you get closer to your five-year vision. Then I want you to start to activate your mind to achieve that goal. The good thing about success is that it is predictable. Success is not an art; it is a science. To win, you need to do four things: 1) know where you are; 2) know where you are going; 3) decide to go; and 4) be persistent in the process. This is why I love the behavioral process, because it's all about getting results and installing new habits in your head that will change your ability to achieve.

– Chapter 6 –

People:
The Influential Process

*When a high achiever steps into any
environment, they want to have more of an impact
on their environment than their
environment has on them.*

This is one of my favorite topics ever to talk about because I believe in it so much. One of the great teachers of leadership is John C. Maxwell, and his philosophy is that leadership is influence. So much of your success can come from being around the right people with the right influence. When you look at the raw definition of influence, it is "the capacity to have an effect on the behavior of someone or something." When talking about mindset, most people don't think of influence at all, but mastering the mind is not just about influencing yourself; it's about the effect you will have on others. This is why I call this important phase the influential process.

When you are influencing yourself and having the right mindset, it affects you, your kids, your coworkers, your employees, your employers, your parents, and pretty much everyone around you. It literally affects every person you come in contact with. When a high achiever steps into any environment, they want to have more of an impact on their environment than their environment has on them. That's the philosophy of influence, and that's the philosophy of the proper mindset. The reason I love the influential process so much is because I love seeing people get break-throughs in their life. I love impacting people around the world.

This is why I even wrote this book, because I hope to influence your thinking. I hope to influence your actions and then influence your results. I remember when I got my first official job as a package runner at NYU Medical Center. I was 16 years old, and this was the first time I felt like I was stepping into man-hood. As I worked this job, there was one person I needed to influence, and that was myself. I needed to influence myself to show up and show up on time, to work hard and have a good attitude. I never really had to think about anyone other than myself. When I became an entrepreneur, this all changed, and it was the first time I had to understand influence. I never really grew up around great leaders. My dad wasn't really around, and I wouldn't call the people in my neighbor-hood the ideal candidates to help me become a profes-sional influencer. Even when I got into business, I got to watch great leaders from a distance, but a lot of what I learned about leadership was by studying people like

John C. Maxwell and others, as well as practicing in real-life situations. Luckily I had some natural leadership gifts from my time in sports. Becoming an entrepreneur is signing up for a crash course in the influential process. If you know me, you know I am not an Ivy League graduate. As a matter of fact, I dropped out of college not once but twice. I never was the smartest, but I understood three things. I understood hard work; I understood the numbers of business; and I understood influencing people. Understanding people has always been my greatest gift and one of the reasons I am where I am today.

There are two types of influences; there are positive ones and negative ones. Most people don't realize this, but everyone influences someone; however, the question is, do you influence them positively or negatively? You should never underestimate the influence you have on others. Whether you think so or not, the way you think, the actions you take, and the results you get impact the people around you, and now with social media, it can affect the greater community. If you want to influence yourself and the world, you must be different than the people you want to influence. You will never influence your environment by trying to be just like it. Let's start with how you can influence yourself both positively and negatively. Then we can talk about how you can influence others.

Five Ways to Influence Yourself Positively

1. Ask the Right Questions

We talked about this earlier, but asking the right questions influences your thinking. Asking the right questions gives you right answers. Asking the right questions forces you to think critically. Asking the right questions pulls out your creativity. Asking the right questions inspires internal reflection. Asking the right questions will challenge your initial assumptions. Asking the right questions forces you to take ownership of solutions instead of focusing on the problem. If you want to influence yourself, one of the first things you must do is make sure you are in control of the thing that controls your thinking.

EVERYONE INFLUENCES SOMEONE

#TheMentalPlaybook
#MentalAsset

How do you ask right questions? There are five ways to ask the right questions:

Five Ways to Influence Yourself Positively

2. Ask the Right Questions

We talked about this earlier, but asking the right questions influences your thinking. Asking the right questions gives you right answers. Asking the right questions forces you to think critically. Asking the right questions pulls out your creativity. Asking the right questions inspires internal reflection. Asking the right questions will challenge your initial assumptions. Asking the right questions forces you to take ownership of solutions instead of focusing on the problem. If you want to influence yourself, one of the first things you must do is make sure you are in control of the thing that controls your thinking. How do you ask right questions? There are five ways to ask the right questions:

A. Become Conscious of Questions You Ask: Most times, people are not even paying attention to what they are saying to themselves. We all know that the way a person thinks could be the controlling factor in their success, so why not be the one in control of that thinking so that you are consciously aware until you grow to a place where if your subconscious took over, it would give you just as good results as your conscious mind.

B. Evaluate the Quality of the Question: If you take the time and think about the words you say to yourself and evaluate whether they are empowering or disempowering, you will start to ask yourself the right questions more often.

C. Frame the Question for Proper Context: Sometimes there is nothing wrong with the question but the context in which the question is being asked. This means looking at the circumstances and asking the questions based on what is happening now and not what happened in the past or what you wish were happening now.

D. Be Intentional about the Outcome of the Answer Before You Ask the Question: If you know you want an empowering answer, understand that before you ask the question. Sometimes if you don't check your attitude, you could be giving yourself improper outcomes before you've even asked the question.

E. Write Answers So That You Can Quantify and Reorganize Better Answers: I know we are in the land of technology, so when I say write something, I sound old, but you don't have to physically write it. You can type it. The most important thing is to get your idea out of your head and in a place where you can see it visually. Seeing the question visually increases your chances of answering it correctly by 45 percent.

2. Proper Focus

Having the proper focus is key to influencing yourself. When you have the proper focus, you can influence how you respond and what you do. Most people don't realize that focus is the gateway thinking, and you can't maximize efficiency without focus, which is why it has such a great positive influence on what we do. There are three ways to have better focus:

A. **Declutter Your Mind:** This just means to stop thinking about things that don't bring you value.

B. **Declutter Your Technology:** Technology is important but not more important than your ability to focus. It's okay to put the phone down every once in a while.

C. **Declutter Your Work Space:** There are a few people who can work in chaos, but most people can't, so be sure to take the time to have a clear work space. This gives you the ability to have a clear mind space and more focus.

When mastering focus, you should focus on these 4P's. These 4P's embody people who perform, process, stay present, and achieve productivity:

<u>Perform</u> - optimal performance

<u>Process</u> - focus on objectives not outcomes

<u>Present</u> - be present in the here and now

<u>Productivity</u> - blocking out distractions increases productivity

3. Listen to Yourself

There is power in intuition, and to be honest, I trust my intuition over anything else. Intuition is one of the things I have built my success on. Remember, your mind is always trying to protect your body subconsciously, so if your subconscious is giving you hints, you should probably take them. Intuition is like sickness. Your body reacts to your mind telling it that something is wrong, and then the mind tells the body what to do and how to handle the problem, sometimes without you even knowing. Most people's intuition is shaped by their past experiences and their current knowledge. Here are three steps to master your intuition:

A. **Pay Attention to How You Feel; Don't Ignore It.** Listening to that gut feeling is the beginning of knowing your intuition.

B. **Ask Yourself Lots of Questions.** The more questions you ask the more your mind will start to guide you to the right decisions. (As you can see, I am all about this asking questions thing; it's kind of a big deal.)

C. **Get Aligned with Your Core Values.** Your intuition always sides with your core values. Follow your intuition, and by default, you will be following your core values.

4. Growth

When trying to positively influence yourself, one of the biggest forms of influence is your own self-development. I am who I am today because of my commitment to self-development. I have heard trainers talk about going on a mental fast for 30 days, where you listen to nothing but personal development for the entire 30 days. Well I went on a five-year mental fast. From 2006 to 2011, I could count on my hands the number of times I chose listening to anything but self-development. I got a little less obsessive in 2012, and part of that is because I met my wife at that time and she balanced me out a bit. Still to this day, 80 percent of what I listen to is self-development. This is a simple concept, but the more you focus on growth the more you will influence how you think, how you feel, what you do, the results you get, and the people you move. Growth is not a "nice to have"; it is the price that must be paid at the counter of success. You don't become more because you want more. Most people don't deserve more influence because they haven't focused on becoming more influential.

How you can grow:
- Get the Books
- Get Mentors

- Get in the Right Environments
- Get the Right Associations
- Go to the Seminars
- Watch the Videos
- Go to the Classes
- Get the Experiences

5. Having a Vision

My vision for my life positively influences all my decision-making, and without a vision, your future becomes bleak. A lot of people are trying to hit a target that was never set. We must understand that forward motion without vision is impossible.

Your vision for your life should inspire you to master all the processes of mastering the mind that we have talked about so far. How do you create vision that influences you to take action? What you want to do is think five years into the future. I don't want you to write out specifics, but I want you to think about what you wish your life would look like five years from now.

MOST PEOPLE DON'T DESERVE MORE INFLUENCE BECAUSE THEY HAVEN'T FOCUSED ON BECOMING MORE INFLUENCIAL

#TheMentalPlaybook
#MentalAsset

Write down a day in the life of you five years from now. What do you wake up doing? Where do you live? Who are you married to? Do you have kids, and how old are they? What is happening around you? What have you accomplished? Once you have laid out a vision that inspires you, ask yourself, what are the most crucial one to three things you can do in the next 12 months to help you get to that five-year vision statement? What are one, two, or three goals that if you focused on them, they would lead you to your five-year vision statement? This vision should inspire you to influence everything you do every day, and if it doesn't, you need to go back and rewrite it until you find something that will motivate you.

Holding on to those five things will positively influence you to do everything you need to do to be everything you desire to become. With every positive, there is a negative; with every up, there is a down. There is something you can do, which a lot of people catch themselves doing, that can negatively influence your success or lack thereof. What are the five negative influences?

Five Ways to Influence Yourself Negatively

1. Holding On to the Past

The past will never be a catalyst to get you to your future. Your past is just a teacher of what worked and what didn't work; it is not a dictator of future outcomes. So many people let the past influence who they are in the present and in the future. Holding on to the past creates negative mindsets and reinforces mistakes you have made. The one thing I want to drill into people is that mistakes of the past are not bad. I don't think they should be forgotten; they should be learned from, but they shouldn't define you. Your past is what happened to you not who you are, so learning to let go will allow you to walk away from the identity you were gaining by holding on to it. Here is how you let go of the past.

How to Let Go of the Past

Step 1: Accept it: Understand that it has happened and there is nothing you can do about it. It is what it is.

Step 2: Be Grateful: Be grateful for your past experiences because there are a lot of people in the world who haven't even lived long enough to have experienced what you experienced. When people realize how much of a gift life is, they won't complain about the fact that they got a chance to live it.

Step 3: Love the Process: Understand that whatever you went through in the past, you needed to go through in order to be the person you were destined to be. Each past experience is a part of the process that develops you into the person you need to be. I have a program call the 4 D's to Destiny, where I really spend a lot of time talking about the process and using the process to get to your destiny.

Step 4: Make New Successful Memories: The great thing about still being alive is the fact that as long as you are alive, you can make new great memories that serve you. You can always draw a line in the sand and say, once I step over this line, I don't look back and I don't go back. Be 100 percent focused on being the person you most want to be instead of focusing on the person you used to be.

2. Lose Touch with Reality

The second way you can influence yourself negatively is if you lose touch with reality. It's interesting to see how people respond to the things that happen to them in life. Sometimes I think people have forgotten what reality looks like. The reality of life is that bad things happen, and you must accept that. You must accept that you're not perfect. You must accept that people will do you wrong. You must accept that people will talk about you. You must accept that people will not believe in you. You must accept that things won't go your way. You must accept that you will fail, but also accept that you will succeed if you don't give up. Accept that your dreams will come true. Accept that your current circumstances do not have to equal your future. All these things are reality, and you are kidding yourself if you don't believe that all of these things will happen someday for you.

3. Not Investing in You

This, to me, is the biggest of the negative influences on yourself. The great Jim Rohn said, "Never begrudge the money you spend on your own personal education." I have literally spent hundreds of thousands (no exaggeration) of dollars on my education, investing in myself. Every dollar I ever spent on me was worth it and has paid for itself 10 times over. Take away my home, and I can get another. Take away my cars, and I can get more. But take away my education, and I would be lost. I wouldn't be where I am now without it.

I have never met an actor, businessman, politician, athlete, or anyone who has achieved on a high level who said that they did not invest in themselves. I heard that LeBron James spends $1.5 million on keeping his body in tip-top championship condition. This is someone who understands the value of investing in themselves. I want to congratulate you on even buying this book because this is a form of investing in yourself. I encourage you to do this one thing: Spend as much as you realistically can on becoming who you want to be.

4. How You Feel

Not paying attention to how you feel can and will negatively influence you. The great thing is, you have the power to change how you feel at any moment, making sure you constantly keep checking the way you feel and that it's not influencing you negatively. If the way you feel is negative, then to change the way you feel, you must change your state, and to change your state, you must do three things:

1. Focus on What Things Mean: What story do you tell yourself?

2. Follow Rituals: What do you do habitually, and does it make you feel positive?

3. Have Movement: There is no change of feeling until you change an action.

5. Negative, Unchanging Routine

Your negative routines can create negative habits that influence you negatively. Even having routines that don't change can influence you negatively. It's important to change up your routine at times. When you change your routine up, you give your brain a chance to be creative, and more importantly, you get to improve your routine and increase your efficiency. All routines are like milk—they are good for a while, and then they go bad. You also get to learn new skills and habits when you do things differently. When you change your routine, you get to identify what part of the routine you don't like and what part doesn't work so that you aren't doing things you hate or aren't efficient just for the sake of being on that routine.

How to Change Routine from Negative to Positive

1. Identify the current routine and the outcome you wish to get from that routine.
2. Assess whether you are getting the outcome.
3. If not, consider tweaks that can be made or change the routine entirely.
4. Plan a new routine and pinpoint the outcome.
5. Set up 30-day challenges that will inspire you to use this new routine to the fullest.
6. Find accountability because getting help is always a positive.

Understanding what influences yourself positively and negatively is incredibly important. It can drive some of the most productive and efficient success you have ever had. Now let's talk about influencing others. I am not going to spend a ton of time on this, but if you want a full breakdown of a four-hour leadership training that I have done, you can get access to my audio program: The Leadership Blueprint. In that audio, I go into depth on the to-do and not-to-do of influence and leadership. I honestly believe that it is some of my best training. Here I want to give you some simple things you can implement right now to better influence others. Let's talk about how you can negatively and positively influence others.

Five Ways to Positively Influence Others

1. Trust

Always think of influencing others like a relationship with a significant other. If you don't have trust in a relationship, then you don't have anything. As a matter of fact, I'm going to say something really radical: I believe trust in a relationship is more important than love. If you are trying to influence someone, you need to be on the same page with them. No one will continue or start a relationship with someone they don't trust. Trust builds reliability, safety, commitment, and value. When you have trust, people will follow you to the ends of the earth, but the moment that trust starts to fade or is broken, that is the beginning of the end of your influence in that relationship. Here is what you need to look out for when building trust:

A. Monitor the Use of the Word *I* When Communicating: In building relationships, the word *I* is self-serving. Going back to the significant-other comparison, if you have a wife or husband and when talking about the relationship, it's all about *I* and not *we*, then you make it about just you and not both parties. This saying *we* has become such a habit that even if I do something by myself, I still say *we*. It doesn't matter if it's for work or personal home situations—I constantly use the word *we*.

B. View Promises as Unpaid Debt: Trust is hard to get and easy to lose. One of the quickest ways to lose trust is by breaking promises, especially when the promises are very important. You can go into what I call relationship bankruptcy if you make promises that you don't live up to. Like bankruptcy, it could take years for you to gain that trust back again.

C. Realize That Your Reputation Is Everything: The start of trust in most relationships comes from your reputation, which is why it's rare for a significant-other relationship to start with two people not knowing each other at all and meeting in random places, like a coffee shop or a club. Relationships have started that way, but it's rare because the woman or guy has to first be 100 percent certain that you are not a serial killer before they can build a friendship much less a relationship. More often than not, relationships get started when you meet through friend introductions, workplace environments, or somewhere that you can verify the trust worthiness of the person.

D. Lying Is an Influence Killer: You can spend your entire life building up your reputation as a trusted source, and one lie can break all that you have built. It's hard to trust someone you don't believe is telling you the truth. We see this in politics all the time, which is why the approval rates for politicians are under 15 percent. It's because, how can you feel comfortable following someone if you can't believe what they are telling you?

E. Learn to Be Positive No Matter Your Mood: This is more of a subtle thing but very important when influencing others. You must learn to manage and monitor your mood. If you are not feeling great, had a bad day, or are just plain upset, you cannot transfer that frustration onto the people you want to influence.

No one can trust a person fully when they don't know who that person is going to be when they see them. If the people I wanted to influence never knew the mood I was going to be in and I transferred that mood to them in every meeting, that would be very unsettling.

F. Build a Fortress of Safety: When parenting, you know that the trust of a child is built on the safety the parent provides. The child doesn't know anything about positive moods, lying, reputations, or promises. That child instinctively knows one thing, and that one thing is that this person is going to keep me safe. When building trust, building a safe environment is key. The safer a relationship feels the closer you feel to the person and the more you trust that person. The reason we move someone from a friend to a best friend is because of the amount of trust we have for that person.

Now that you know what to look out for when building trust with the people you want to influence, let's talk about the strategies to increase your trust with people.

Listen First: The old saying is that you have two ears and one mouth for a reason—so you can listen twice as much as you speak. If you are the one desiring to have the influence when building this trust, you must be the one willing to listen first. By listen, I mean really listen, not just listen so you know how and with what to respond. Listening will give you all the information you need in order to know what is important to the person. It also gives you the ability to know what that person cares about because if you care about what they care about, they care about what you care about. This is the foundation of trust.

Talk Straight: Being upfront is a lost art. In today's politically correct world, everyone talks in roundabout ways, never really getting to the point of what they really want to say. A lot of times, it's because of them being scared of what they really want to say, and that's understandable but inefficient. When you talk in roundabout ways, it sounds like you are hiding something and makes people suspicious of your real intentions. I used to do this all the time. I used to ask questions to set up the real question, and I had to learn that if you do that, it always makes a person feel like you are hiding something. If you have teenage kids, you see this often, when the kid asks one question and you know they really want to know something else. Teenager asks, "Dad, are you doing anything Saturday." Dad says, "I am not sure, why?" Teenager says, "Well I was just thinking about going out with some friends tomorrow morning." Then the dad says, "Great, go have fun." Then the teenager asks, "So Dad, are you not going out Saturday?" and the dad asks, "What does me going out have to do with you?" Then the teenager finally says what they really wanted: "So Dad, can I borrow your car?" The car was what they wanted from the beginning, and when it's your parents, you can get away with things like that, but when you want to build trust with people, that form of not being direct just makes you sound shady. I had to learn this the hard way.

Be Transparent: I don't think there is anything that can help you build more trust than being transparent. People love people who are willing to be open and up-front about themselves. Being transparent shows you have nothing to hide, and showing you have nothing to hide shows that you can be trusted. Trust is one of those things you give first and then expect in return. Being transparent with someone allows them to see that if you were willing to trust me, I can trust you.

Have Clear Expectations: When you enter into any type of relationship, if the expectations of that relationship are not clear from the beginning, things can break down quickly. If someone is expecting you to be or do things that you don't exactly do, then you, in essence, are breaking an agreement that was not even officially made. I see this happen between people all the time, where one person expected something that the other person didn't, and they lose trust for that person because they feel like they didn't keep their end of the deal. It is important to have the deal clear from day one.

Extend Trust: I mentioned this briefly when I talked about being transparent. When you want trust, you must give it—no ifs or maybes about this. No one trusts unless trusted, and no one is trusted unless they trust. Trust is one of those mutually extended actions that can only be displayed on one end when it is displayed on the other. It's like a seesaw—the seesaw can only go up on one side when there is weight on the other, and vice versa.

Right Your Wrongs Quickly: The greatest influencers are those who make mistakes, like we all do, but own up to them quickly. People understand that no one is perfect, but when you compound a mistake by another and another, and you don't admit when you are wrong, you lose people's trust. People have respect and trust for those who take responsibility for their mistakes and apologize. Now this doesn't mean you can keep making the same mistake and apologizing for it over and over again. There is a point where people will feel like you are not sincere, and it will have the opposite effect because if you really were sorry, you would change your actions. If you don't change, then people no longer trust your apologies.

Give Respect: This one is very simple. If you don't respect someone, why would they trust you? Giving someone basic human respect as a person is key to gaining their trust. The opposite of respect is disrespect. Who would trust a person who is disrespectful to them? Much less, who would even like a person who doesn't respect them?

Get Better: If you are influencing someone, you must get better today than you were yesterday. This is what allows someone to continue to trust you. If you are constantly making the same mistakes and not growing, people will start to lose trust for you.

Be Loyal: Loyalty goes a long way in trust. Most trust relationships break because of a lack of loyalty to the person you are supposed to trust. This happens when you tell someone something personal that was supposed to be between you and them, and they tell others. That is you no longer being loyal to that person; it's breaking their trust.

Deliver Results: The more you deliver results the more you trust someone. I learned this lesson with my wife. When I told her I was going to do something and I delivered, her trust in me increased, and every time I deliver results, her trust increases. Before when I told her what I was going to do, she wanted to know how I was going to do it, and now I tell her what I am going to do and she just knows it's going to get done because she trusts that I have delivered in the past, and that means I should deliver in the future. This is exactly how credit reports work. They base your score on your ability to pay your bills in the past, and that's how they know if they can trust you with another loan in the future.

2. Care

If you want to influence people positively, you must care first. The old and mostly overused statement is, people don't care how much you know until they know how much you care. This is actually not a necessity of influence because you know a ton of celebrities who might have influence on you and you know they don't care about you. If you become a person who cares, you have 10 times the ability to influence—even if it's just the image of caring from a distance. When Taylor Swift shows up at one of her fans' houses with Christmas gifts and records, even if it wasn't your house, you would feel like she was one of the few celebrities who cared.

Whether you are a fan of hers or not, most people know that she has millions of fans, so most would say she must care if she takes the time to do that, even though you know it's impossible for her to care for all the millions of them, but the act gives the image of caring at scale. A lot of people think you can't scale caring for that many people, but with technology today and things like social media, that becomes possible now. Deep caring equals deep influence. If you want people to move mountains for you, be willing to move mountains for them. When you show that you care, you show someone you are not selfish, which allows people to open up and feel like you have their best interest at heart. Here is how you show you care:

Go Above and Beyond to Help Them Personally: When you do things that people know you don't have to do for them, you show that you care for them as a person. Doing more than necessary shows you really care.

Never Prop Yourself above Them: When you care about someone, you do not make yourself more important than them. Caring for someone says you see them as an equal.

Show Interest in the Things They Care About: Caring about their family, friends, and hobbies, and showing interest in them lets them know you care.

Make Time for Them: When people say they haven't had time for a person, what they are really saying is that they haven't cared about them as much as they care about the other things going on in their life. This is okay; caring has different levels. I am sure there are people you care about and don't talk to daily, but there are certain people you have a priority to care about. There is no excuse for you not to talk to your wife, husband, or kid for years. Making time for a person really shows you care.

Have Their Back in Times of Trouble: When things get rough, that's when you start to see who is for you and who is against you. When people turn their backs from helping you in the worst possible times, it is an indication that they never really cared about you in the first place. When times are tough and you are going through it, you should be able to rely on the people you think are in your corner. If they aren't in your corner because you are down, they should have never been in your corner in the first place.

3. Confidence

If you are going to influence anyone, you must have confidence. I am going to talk more about confidence later in the book, but we must understand that timidity is not a virtue. Timid people are not respected because they are looked at as weak. I have no problem with timid people, but the world looks at timid people as non-achievers. Our society is built on the idea of the hero, the conqueror. Timid people are not known as conquerors. Have you ever watched Superman? Have you ever wondered why no one ever knew Clark Kent was Superman? I mean, their bodies are built the exact same. They look the same, basically the same hair, same height, and same weight. The only thing that is different is the glasses, but when people saw Clark, they saw a timid, shy guy, and no matter how much they look similar, people couldn't believe the timid guy could be a hero. That is why Clark never had influence like Superman. Most people don't succeed because they are afraid. The people who influence and inspire are the ones with seemingly no fear, the ones with the confidence to take over the world. A confident person takes action and believes in themselves, and that belief is crucial to influencing others.

There are many ways to build confidence, and I am going to give you my three most powerful ways:

Change Your Body Language and Image: If you look at someone, and they have their head down, are sad, and look defeated, would you say this person is glowing with confidence? Of course not, but if the person stands straight up, looking at you with eye contact and a smile, you would say this person is confident. Your body language and the image you walk around with show your confidence or lack thereof.

Preparation: A great way to build and show confidence is by being prepared. If you are prepared, then when you step into situations where you need confidence, you will always have it. When you are not prepared, how can you be confident? If you have spent the time in practice and growth, then when you step out into the real-life situations, you can have the confidence as if you have been there and done that before.

Positive Expectations: When you expect to win, you have the confidence of a winner. If you expect to lose, then you lack that confidence. Learning to always have positive expectations helps you influence the masses. Having an expectation to win doesn't mean you always will, but it means you believe you always will, and believing is the beginning of confidence.

THE PEOPLE WHO INFLUENCE AND INSPIRE ARE THE ONE WITH SEEMINGLY NO FEAR

#TheMentalPlaybook
#MentalAsset

4. Consistency

You can't build positive influence in a day, a week, or a month. Influence is built over time, and there are very few times when that statement is broken. There may be a time when someone has gained influence in front of millions of people in an instant—for example, if they have a video that goes viral or if they are endorsed by an influential person. The difference between a one-hit wonder or someone with 15 minutes of fame and the person who has put in consistent work to be great over time is that the person who put in the time is ready for the spotlight and has developed the skills necessary to stay in the spotlight and be great. The ones who were luckily seen by the masses without putting in the time to be great usually don't stick around long. If you consistently prepare for the moment and have skills, you deserve to be on top in the moment, and if you didn't consistently prepare, it will just be 15 minutes of fame. Consistency is the thing that develops your reputation. Over time, people know who you are, the value you bring, and why you do it. This allows you to be an influence to the people around you. Consistency also allows you to maintain a message that people can trust. They can trust who you say you are because you have been that person over time. One of the most important facts of consistency is that it builds momentum. Momentum is a force you want on your side. We have talked about habit in this book, and consistency builds strong positive habits. Consistency also shows character and shows you are not a quitter. It shows that you are not a flash-in-the-pan success. All these things contribute to your influence. There are rules to building consistency.

Building Consistency Rules

Rule #1: Focus on the end goal not the process. The process is a part of the journey, but when you focus on the end vision, the end goal, it gives you the inspiration to continue to be consistent.

Rue #2: Build rituals that allow for you to stay consistent. The more rituals you have in place the easier it is to stay consistent.

Rue #3: Act in spite of how you feel. You will never feel like doing the right thing all the time. When there are times you don't feel like doing the consistent action, you must take action anyway.

Rule #4: Get into the right environment for success. Environment plays a big part in success and consistency. Try to create environments that help you build consistency and not environments that change your being consistent.

Rule #5: Have a plan and decide. Once you have decided that you want to be consistent, you must have a clear process in getting to the end result. If you fail to plan, then you plan to fail.

5. Knowledge

There is no influence without knowledge. You don't have to be knowledgeable about everything if you want to influence. You just need to be knowledgeable about the things you want to influence people on. Knowledge is the prerequisite for influence. It's one of the first things people look for when deciding if someone is worthy of influencing them. One of the first things I learned from Jim Rohn was, ignorance is not bliss. Ever since that day, I have been on the quest to absorb as much knowledge as possible. I truly believe that the beginning gateway of success is knowing. Before I started my journey of success, I didn't know. I didn't know how to think; I didn't know the best things to do; and I didn't know what was possible. The change in my life was when I went from not knowing to knowing. When I talk about getting knowledge, I'm not just talking about reading, seminars, audios, and stuff like that. Yes, those things are necessary, but there is one thing more necessary than those, and that is patience. To be knowledgeable, you must be patient. No one is a genius from birth. They may learn fast, but they must take the time to learn. Being world class at anything takes time. In your quest for knowledge, don't be so focused on the getting of information; be focused on becoming the information you receive. Amateurs focus on getting information, and professionals focus on becoming the information they get. Getting the information is like doing a crash-course study for a school exam. Becoming the information is knowing it so well that you can't forget it. Once you get and become information and you have the knowledge, at that point, you can be a person of influence. It's not just because you went to some fancy school or training but because you went to the trainings, applied what the training taught, and became the person the trainings told you that you could become. That is influence at its highest level.

Now that I have given you the five things you need to positively influence others, let me give you the four things that negatively influence others. These four things can make you lose the influence you have built or are building:

1. Being Rude or Egotistical

Having ego is the easiest way to lose influence. Treating people like crap is the fastest route to get them not to like you. You see this happen often, when people get to a certain amount of success and start to treat others as if they are not important. Ego makes you a selfish person who doesn't listen and is defensive. Having an ego is not always bad, but the way most people display ego is not in the constructive way. Don't let your ego knock you out of influence.

2. Being Argumentative

No one likes to lose an argument, and in every argument, someone wins and someone loses. If you constantly argue with people, you will always start to erode your influence. If you have ever had the problem of being able to have success and influence outside the house but can never influence your spouse in the same way, this is because there are too many back-and-forth exchanges. Arguing makes it you versus them instead of you and them. It's impossible to influence someone you're constantly fighting with.

3. Lacking Belief

If you don't believe, then you don't have the ability to influence. Most people are influenced by you because they believe in you, but if you don't believe in yourself, how do you expect someone else to believe in you? Belief gives you the courage to take a step and to blaze the trail. If you don't believe, you don't take a step. If you don't take a step, there is no trail to blaze and no one to follow behind you. Belief is key!

4. Complaining

Nobody wants to be around a complainer, much less be led by one. How can you influence anyone to be better when you can't even influence yourself to be better? Complaining and excuse-making are the epitome of failure personified. A person who's complaining says, I don't have the power to make the changes I want to make to live the life I want to live. Complaining is a disease that can affect any willing host. I try my best not to be around complainers because what they have is contagious.

In the influential process, we talked about how to influence yourself and others positively and negatively, but now let me tie this into the Mental Matrix. Like I said earlier, a lot of people don't understand how influence plays a part in the conversation of mindset. When you think about the largest influencers in the world, they have that influence because of their ability to get results: Michael Phelps, Martin Luther King Jr., LeBron James, Mother Teresa, Denzel Washington, Beyoncé, Michael Jackson, President Barack Obama,

Steve Jobs, Bill Gates. No matter the industry, their influence comes from their ability to get results. I call these people high achievers. The skills that these types of people have are great. They have vision, faith, leadership, communication, intuition, innovation, forward thinking, and so much more. The world turns because of influential people like these. This influence falls into two categories, poverty and prosperity.

Remember that when I say prosperity, I am not just talking about money. Prosperity to me is flourishing, thriving, and succeeding at anything you do. Poverty is the state of being inferior in quality or being insufficient in amount. Prosperity is influence, success, achievement, well-being, positivity, plenty, wealth, affluence, opulence, the good life, happiness, joy, love, friendship, family, and being spiritually awake. Poverty is fear, anxiety, worry, doubt, lack, hurt, pain, loneliness, despair, selfishness, envy, jealousy, hardship, need, insufficiency, absence, shortage, purposelessness, and death.

How can you influence the world in poverty? This is why we strive for prosperity and for impact. It's why I do what I do. I work hard. I sacrifice. I do today what others don't for one word above all, and that word is *legacy*. I want to know that before I leave this earth, I did something worthwhile. I didn't waste my time on this planet, focused on things that didn't make any impact on my family, my purpose, and my dreams to make this world better because I was here.

The reason we ask the right questions to get the right answers, to have the right thoughts, to think the right way so our bodies can make the proper actions, to build positive state, actions, and habits is to live a life of prosperity. It's all to live a life of prosperity and to become, to achieve, and to get the results we want and live a life of influence. As you use this framework of Mental Matrix to create results and a life of prosperity, I pray that you use your influence for good and not for evil. The world is counting on you to become the most influential person you can possibly be. Once you have this influence, you must use it to make a positive impact in the world.

– Chapter 7 –

Mission:
The Crusade Process

We don't let the enemy destroy us; we destroy the enemy.

My goal has always been to inspire a group of crusaders who are willing to fight for their dreams, their goals, and their purpose in life. In order to do this, you must be willing to fight the opinions and negative mindset of the world. I get fired up thinking about all the people who told me I wouldn't amount to anything, all the people who said I was just a statistic, and that principal who said I would be dead or in jail by 21. When I think about all the people I have ever coached and all the negative mindsets they had to battle to reach success, it lights a fire under me.

There are people out there trying to kill dreams, trying to squash visions and destroy your hope. As long as I am alive, I will fight this negative mindset. I have been fighting these negative mindsets my entire life, battling against the thoughts of other people who had a lack of belief in themselves and pushed that lack of belief onto me. Through this fight, I have learned to be a crusader, and I started building crusaders who are battling those negative mindsets in their own life. What I love about crusaders is that they die hard. We don't let the enemy destroy us; we destroy the enemy.

This is one of the keys to mastering the mind, knowing that the mind is under attack. The mind has been locked in chains due to the way society works. Our minds have been put in captivity, but the truth is that most people don't know their mind has been put in captivity because it looks like they're free. It's like the zoo, and you're a lion.

The habitat looks similar to your natural-born habitat, but you are still imprisoned. I am crusading for the lion in your mind to expand past the zoo you have been imprisoned in—to help you realize you belong in the wild, where there is unlimited potential, where you can do what you want, go where you want, and become what you want. We have all been birthed and designed for prosperity, but the world has been programming you for poverty. I am on a crusade to reverse that programming and remind you to think like the lion you were born to be.

Your mind is like the lion because it is king of its domain. When you look at lions in the jungle, you have to ask yourself, why are they king of the jungle?

AS
LONG
AS
I AM
ALIVE
I WILL
FIGHT
THIS
NEGATIVE
MIDSET

#TheMentalPlaybook
#MentalAsset

They are not the smartest in the jungle—that's probably the chimpanzee or the hyena. They are not the strongest in the jungle—that's the elephant. They are not the tallest in the jungle—that's the giraffe. They are not the largest in the jungle—that's probably the hippopotamus. They are not even the fastest—that's the cheetah. So why the heck are lions king of the jungle? They are the king because they think they are the king. They are the king because of their mindset. It's not ability, and it's never been ability. It has and will always be the mentality that creates success.

When the lion sees the elephant, what comes to the lion's mind? It is not that the elephant is so big or so strong. No, the thing that comes to the lion's mind when he sees the elephant is "lunch." Elephants are 10 times stronger, heavier, and more power, but when the lion sees the elephant, none of that matters. The lion's mindset is lunch. The lion thinks he can eat the elephant, and the most important thing is not just that the lion thinks this way. It is because the lion acts the way he thinks. Because he thinks he can eat the elephant, he attacks the elephant. When the elephant sees the lion, even with the elephant's greater abilities, the elephant sees the lion and thinks, "Oh no! Attacker!" The elephant is controlled by his thinking, and he thinks he is "lunch." Therefore, all his abilities are useless because of the way he thinks. His authority is imprisoned by his mindset.

Everyone allows the world to tell them they are not strong enough, are not smart enough, don't have enough money, didn't grow up in the right place, or didn't have the right parental upbringing. People buy this crappy thinking. They don't realize these things mean nothing when it comes to achieving. The beginning of achievement is not abilities; it's mindset. When the mindset is strong, you can build your abilities to be stronger. You can have strong abilities and negative mindset and still fail, but you will never have strong mindset and fail regardless of abilities. I know people with fewer abilities than others but are running circles around them in achievement because of their mind. This is why I call myself a crusader. This is why I am looking to build crusaders who are on a mission to kill negative mindsets—crusaders with the mindset of

King Leonidas in the movie *300*. In the movie, King Leonidas and his army of 300 were walking to battle, and they met up with some potential allies who wanted to join forces with them. The leader of the potential allies saw that King Leonidas only had 300 men with him and got upset because he had thousands with him. He said to King Leonidas, "I thought you were committed to battle. Why did you bring so little soldiers?" King Leonidas then started pointing to men in the allies' army and asking them what they do for a living. The men said everything from bakers to potters. Then King Leonidas turned to his men and asked, "Spartans, what is your profession?" The Spartans all howled in several fearsome bellows in reply. Then King Leonidas stated to the potential allies, "It looks like, my friend, that I have actually brought more soldiers than you."

I tell this story because when you have the mind set of King Leonidas, you know what you come to the table with. You know your strength and your potential. You won't let any negative mind tell you anything different. I am not crusading to make a living. I can spend my time doing other things that could make more money. I build crusaders to make an impact in the lives of future crusaders and build an environment where my kids can grow up not be inundated with negative mindsets. Our kids and our future generations are being tainted by the negative mindsets, from the media, from their friends and neighbors, from social media. Ninety-five percent of the population thinks in a way that doesn't allow them to be people of influence and live in prosperity. Most people's thinking will lead them down a path to poverty. I am here to change that. I want to play a part, even if it's just a little part, in driving that number down and inspiring a generation of crusaders determined to kill the negative mindset.

The greatest paycheck I will ever receive is the paycheck of joy I get just to be a part of a movement to fight the fight and inspire others to fight the fight and save their family. Changing the way you think can turn over a new leaf in your family tree and change the impact your family name can have on the world. I didn't grow up with the mindset of achieving. I didn't grow up learning this stuff. My son will. His son will. And I pray that his sons and daughters will. We will change it in our family tree, in our community, and in any person's life we encounter.

Being a Crusader Is Three Things to Me:

1. Creating the prosperity mindset, the achiever's mindset, and using the Mental Matrix to help others master the mind.
2. Helping others fight the negative mindsets in themselves, their family, and those they encounter.
3. Inspiring others to fight the negative mindset in themselves, their family, and those they encounter.

I have spoken a lot in this chapter about fighting the negative mindset, but how do you do that? How do you battle the negative mindset in yourself and in the ones who try to put the negative mindset on you? There are four things you can do to fight the negative mindset.

HIS AUTHORITY IS IMPRISONED BY HIS MINDSET

#TheMentalPlaybook
#MentalAsset

Fighting the Negative Mindset

1. Pay Attention to Negative Thought Patterns: Most people never even notice the negative thoughts that they have or receive from others. You must not just notice them; you must kill them right away. Negative thoughts serve no real purpose and will directly cause unproductive results—negative thoughts, like anxiousness, worry, criticism, self-beating, regret, and guilt. None of these thoughts serve you. A lot of fighting the negative thoughts is twofold, asking yourself the right questions and being consciously in the moment. Most people never take the time to think about what they are doing and how they're thinking. If you can take the time and pay attention when the negative surfaces, you can take steps to kill it. The first step to fighting this enemy is knowing it exists.

2. Be Unidentified with Negative Thinking: One of the biggest things I see when I am coaching people is not just that they think negatively about them-selves but about what they can and can't do, and

who they are and aren't. Most people associate negative thought as their identity. You can't identify with the negativity because it can not only damage you in the moment but can damage long-term. This happened with me when that principal said I would be dead or in jail by 21. What that principal said became my identity, and for years, I lived someone else's identity for me. The identity that you take up may even be true for the moment. Someone might say, well you're fat, or broke, or you come from a broken home, or whatever, and that may be true, but your current situation does not dictate your identity. The situation you're in is not who you are.

You may be fat now, but you don't have to identify with that by saying things like, "I'm big-boned." No, if you don't want to be fat anymore, you can choose to be fit and turn your identity from "I am fat" to "I am on my way to being fit." You may be broke, and I have been there, but you cannot identify with being broke. I used to say, "I'm not broke. My money is just in circulation." It's all about your perspective on the negative thinking. If you decide to take on negative thinking as your identity, you are dead in the water before you even start. You must learn to give up the victim role. You are not a victim; you are a victorious crusader.

3. Double Down on the Positive: When negative happens, people tend to give it so much attention. As a matter of fact, people give it more attention than it generally deserves. They highlight it, talk about it, listen to songs about it, and write poetry about it. Most people dwell in the place of negativity. They are in a storm, and instead of fighting through the storm, they grab a bed and sleep in the middle of the storm. When something good happens, they pay very little attention to it. They don't take the time to celebrate, pat themselves on the back, or identify with the positive. Most people don't identify with the positive, but I urge you to double down on positive anytime you have a chance to.

When something positive happens, identify with it. Don't let the moment go without embracing it and accepting it as the life you want. Remember, what you focus on grows, so focus on what you want. Also you must stop waiting for something positive to happen to you in order for you to focus on positive. You have to find positive in all situations. I was talking to a friend of mine, and she was saying she was happy because she got something she wanted. I asked her how she would have felt if she didn't get what she wanted, and she said she would've been sad. She then asked me what made me happy.

My answer to her was, I wake up. She was confused, and I said that the only thing that makes me happy is, I wake up. If you have to get, have, or become something in order to be happy, then your happiness will always be out of your control. If you don't have those things, you can't be happy. I always teach people to learn to just be happy with life, and as you get those things, let them add a bit more joy to your life, but don't let them make you miserable if you don't have them. This is one of the best ways to double down on the positive. Find ways to double down on the positive, and see positive as anything and everything.

4. Stop Believing in Fear: To fight negative thinking, you have to stop believing in fear. Trying to fight negative thinking and believing in fear is like trying to fight a war and supplying your enemy with all their weaponry. I remember a movie I watched, *After Earth* with Will Smith, and he had an amazing line where he said, "Fear is not real. The only place that fear can exist is in our thoughts of the future. It is a product of our imagination causing us to fear things that do not at present and may not ever exist. That is near insanity. Do not misunderstand me. Danger is very real, but fear is choice." What a powerful statement! You have the choice, so I ask you, what do you choose?

    You can choose to believe you are a crusader with the ability to achieve everything you have ever dreamed, to live a life in prosperity. Or you can choose to believe in fear, believe that nothing is possible, and instead of a crusader, you are a victim. You are a victim of your circumstance, a victim of your thinking, and destined to live a life of poverty, hopelessness, and despair. The most important thing to know is that you get to choose what you believe in—even if you don't have evidence that the belief you want to believe in is real. That's what the word *faith* is birthed out of. If you decide to believe in your fears, you get to keep them. If you've decided to believe in your dreams, you get to live them.

How does the crusader process fit in with the Mental Matrix? The crusader process is the entire Mental Matrix. The crusader process is like the movie *The Matrix*, one of my favorite movies of all time. And if you watch the movie, you remember that Morpheus says, "What you know, you can't explain, but you feel it. You've felt it your entire life, that there is something wrong with the world. You don't know what it is, but it's there like a splinter in your mind." It is this feeling that has brought you to read this book, master the mind, and fight negative thinking. This is the Matrix. The Mental Matrix is the source. It is the origin of success, all success. It all starts with your thoughts, which are then fed to your mind, which triggers you to behave positively or negatively. This trigger affects your state, your actions, and your habits, which lead to you living your life in fear and poverty or faith and prosperity.

This is a fight against all negative thinking that you can see outside of your window or when you turn on your television. You can feel it when you go to work, even when you go to church. It is the thinking that has been force-fed to you to blind you from the truth. The truth is that you are a slave to your thinking. You were born into bondage, born into captivity. You were born in a prison you can't see, taste, or touch, a prison for your mind. My favorite part of what Morpheus said was, this is your chance. You can take the blue pill. The story ends, and you go back to thinking the way you have been taught to think, staying mentally imprisoned, never achieving the greatness you know you have been destined for. Or you take the red pill. Stay in Wonderland and see how far the rabbit hole goes. See how much you're thinking affects every area of your life and every result that you get.

You have the choice to choose negative thinking and poverty or positive thinking and prosperity. If you choose prosperity, then welcome to the life of a crusader. You become a crusader for your purpose, a crusader for your family, a crusader for the world. You become someone who unplugs from the negative thinking of the world and begins to battle those out there who fight to keep negativity flowing. It's time for you to use this Mental Matrix to master your mind, change your thinking, and become the person you always knew you could be. You are an achiever; you are a victor; you are a crusader. Keep your vision alive and strong. And remember, I'm in your corner, rooting for you. Let's change the world together!

YOU HAVE THE CHOICE TO CHOOSE NEGATIVE THINKING AND POVERTY OR POSITIVE TINKING AND PROSPERITY

#TheMentalPlaybook
#MentalAsset

Part II:

The Achiever's Playbook

This section is about giving you short lessons learned over the course of my journey to winning on a high level. This achiever's playbook is all about giving you the 10 key ways to think that separate the average from the high achiever.

– Chapter 8 –

The BVF Factor

Whether you think you can
or you think you can't,
you're absolutely right.

What is the BVF factor? The BVF factor is the Belief Vision Fear factor. These three things are the motors that make the engine of success run masterfully. The understanding of this principle is the foundation of high achievement. Having control of these three factors is a major separator of the average and the extraordinary. I am sure that upon learning this, a couple of questions come to mind. Why are these factors so important? How do you control them? How do you implement them to separate yourself from the average and become a high achiever?

First, let's start with why these factors are so important. They are important because they dictate what you determine as truth, how far you go, and what you do. Belief is the most important factor. Some would disagree with that, as some believe that vision comes before belief. I believe that there is no compelling vision without belief. Belief determines the size and the impact of your vision. Because of a lack of belief, most people don't have a vision compelling enough to pull them into success. If vision is a house, then belief is the foundation on which that home is built.

BELIEF DETERMINES THE SIZE AND THE IMPACT OF YOUR VISION

#TheMentalPlaybook
#MentalAsset

Most people don't succeed, not because they can't but because they don't believe that they can. One quote I live my life by is, "Whether you think you can or you think you can't, you're absolutely right." The foundation of human society today was built and will continue to be built on the belief of individual ability.

We as a species have constantly pushed beyond what we once believed to be true or limited. Belief is what moves men to do the impossible. Imagine what this world would be if the high achievers didn't believe in themselves and their abilities. Imagine if Benjamin Franklin didn't believe that he had the ability to discover how we can use electricity to increase our standard of living. What if Edison didn't commercialize the light bulb? What about the Wright brothers and the airplane, or Henry Ford and the car, or Charles Babbage, who designed the first computer? All these things took a level of belief that compelled them to create something that eventually changed the world. The ability to believe is a powerful force. Can a bird fly? Is the sky blue? Obvious questions, right? Here is a not-so-obvious question for some. Can you succeed? You can do anything you believe you can.

Here is the problem. Most people believe that somehow these people who succeed are special. The only thing that makes the successful special is that they understand what I'm telling you right now. Now that you're reading this, you have separated yourself from the masses because you now understand it too, that the key separator is belief. Once your belief is solid, you're no longer shackled by doubt, and you can now start to build a vision on that foundation.

A compelling vision, being the second factor, can be the difference between acting on your goals and dreams or remaining stagnant. Vision is a special and important trait. Vision is the art of seeing what's often invisible to others but clear as day to you. It is your job to paint that vision as clearly to others as it is to you. What the successful understand is that no one makes it to a place of success without other people helping and participating along the way. It takes a vision that inspires and motivates those around you to create something magnificent and special. See, you need belief before you have a compelling vision, but the people who follow you need a compelling vision before they can believe. Your vision is like the Pablo Picasso painting, showing everyone what the future looks like if they just lock on to the path you are trailblazing.

Most leaders wonder why their people get weary and quit on the journey. It's because they have no vision of greater pastures to hold on to. A great quote in the Bible says, "Without vision, the people perish." (Proverbs 29:18) It is absolutely true. The ability to cast a compelling vision and get people to buy into that vision for themselves is what separates the average from the super successful. When it comes to vision, here is how people drop the ball. They forget that it's one thing to have a vision, but it's another to help each individual person fit the vision into where they want to go in life. It's important to note that when casting a vision, there are three reasons people get weary on the journey and quit.

First, they might stop believing in the vision itself. Normally this comes from the leader's lack of ability to create results. If you're looking to create massive success and you have people following you (which all super-successful people do), then you have to find a way to win! It's like you're the general of your troops, and every day, every month, and every year, you send them out to battle. If you go battle after battle after battle and never see a major victory, you start to lose soldiers. Some soldiers die off; some tire and give up; some flip sides and join the side of the war that seems to be winning; and the ones who stay out of a sense of loyalty stop actually fighting, even though you see them on the battlefield with you. If they stop believing in the vision, you have to rally them up for one last battle, and in that battle, YOU HAVE TO, YOU HAVE TO, YOU ABSOLUTELY HAVE TO WIN!! Not only do you have to win but you have to win big!

The second reason people get weary on the journey toward your vision and quit is because they still have faith in the vision but lost faith in your ability to guide them down the path of that vision. This happens for a few reasons. Either there's a character and integrity issue, or your path changes on such a constant basis that it seems like you're lost at every turn. No one wants to follow someone who is lost. The super successful understand that character and integrity are a very important part of getting others to follow your vision. If people can't trust you, then they can't trust your vision. If they can't trust your vision, there's no way they can feel confident and walk down the path that you have laid out for them.

If you're dealing with this, you first have to clean up your integrity issues, and I suggest hiring a coach. A coach will point out all of the things that you can't see and keep you focused on the path that will lead you to success. However, in situations where there's an integrity issue, sometimes it's best to just start over. Your past mistakes are in the past, and if I were you, I would work on building a new team of people around you. The reason for this is that when people get hurt, it's hard for them to forgive, and if they don't forgive, they can't get past the mistakes of your past. If you hold on to those people and still bring on new people, you're going to poison the new people with the old people's thinking. Therefore, your best bet is to clean up the character issues and start to build a new team that you can lead. If the issue is that you keep changing, you have to stop. The only way for people to have your vision and allow that vision to go from their head to their heart is if the vision is consistent and persistent. That repetitive vision will burn into the subconscious and be unforgettable. This is how you make the vision a part of them and not just something that they hear.

The last reason you lose people on the journey to your vision is because they stop believing in themselves. This mainly happens when you're developing the vision but not developing the people in that vision. The minute someone believes that they don't have the ability to play a vital role in the vision, you know the vision was casted to them but not developed in them. However, this should be the least likely scenario unless you are bringing the wrong type of people into your organization. If you're hiring people or bringing people along who don't fit the type of person that you should be looking for, then you're asking for trouble in advance. When you're bringing people into your business, organization, or company, you should be looking for those who have high self-esteem, are committed to growth, are relentless, and possess all the other qualities that are important to you as the leader.

If you have the right type of people, it's rare that they stop believing in themselves. Yes, the vision that you cast is for you, but it's more for the people who are following you. The super successful understand that implementing and executing a vision is a major factor in massive success. When you have a strong foundation of belief, when you can create a compelling vision that others can follow, fear is inevitable, but fear is also conquerable.

Fear is the last factor. Fear is something you can't get around, and the super successful know this. The successful do not fear the fear. The average person allows fear to dictate whether they have success or whether they don't, whether they give it their all or nothing at all. Fear is the silent killer choking the dreams and potential out of the masses and reverting them to a life of aimless living and unachieved dreams. If you ever watch the show *Fear Factor*, you know it's a show where they have this big money prize at the end for those willing to do tasks that would frighten even the toughest gladiator. If the task is so frightening, why do people still go on the show? It's because of the compelling vision of what the bucket of money at the end will bring to them. Their belief that the vision is worth it stops their fear of doing that frightening task. If they didn't believe in the vision, then they would never have taken on the task. The ability to have a compelling vision and the ability to have belief in that vision are the ultimate fear destroyers. Would you believe you can do it even if you're afraid of it? The belief in that compelling vision gives you the power. There's a great book titled *Feel the Fear and Do It Anyway* by Susan Jeffers, and if most people took on that philosophy, they would be achieving a lot more goals, visions, and dreams. Jim Rohn said, "When the promise is clear, the price is easy." It's hard to add to Jim Rohn, but I would add to that quote: "Once I believe in the promise and the promise is clear, I will pay the price."

Belief in your ability to achieve the promise will allow you to take action. Most people spend their life running away from the idea of fear. The super successful understand that fear is inevitable, but they believe and have a compelling vision, so their fear doesn't stop them. Some believe it's because they have no fear that they are courageous, but that's not true. The truth is that they have fear and they act in spite of that fear, which is what makes them courageous. Those who are on a journey to become a high achiever are usually closer to that success than they think. Usually the thing holding them back from taking that next step is some fear in their life that they haven't faced or conquered. Understanding the BVF factor and implementing it into your life will put you one step closer to moving from average to a high achiever and becoming super successful. If I were you, before I moving on to the next chapter, I would look at the BVF factor and evaluate my own life.

Asking yourself questions is the key to unlocking your subconscious potential. I would be asking myself, where am I lacking in belief? How can I strengthen my belief in myself, my vision, and my goals? What is my vision? Is my vision compelling to myself and others? Have I properly communicated that vision to others in ways where they would follow me? What fears are holding me back? How do I channel my fears and change them from roadblocks into stepping stones to get me closer to my vision? Those are all important questions to ask yourself in order to allow the BVF factor to work in your life.

– Chapter 9 –

The Insecure One

*What people say or think
about you has less to do with you
and more to do with them.*

As you know, being a kid growing up in the inner city, I found myself hanging out with kids who were prone to getting in trouble. This led me to a destructive path and dealing with a lot of emotion and with what the principal said. I built an uncertainty within myself that shaped me and my decisions. These uncertainties were based on three specific things that began to lead me down a dark path. As I watch people on the journey to go from average to a high achiever, I saw people making the same three mistakes that create a level of insecurity that can block them from becoming successful. These three things, which come with insecurity, can become a disease that if not checked and cured, will kill your chances of becoming great.

The Three Diseases of Insecurity

1. Lack of Confidence

One of the main things you see in someone who is super successful is a confidence that they are comfortable in their own skin—not an arrogance but described as SWAG in urban colloquialism. That confidence shows in the way they walk, the way they talk, and the way they interact with people. They show that they are not beneath everyone, but they also show that they are not above anyone either. It's a confidence that makes people comfortable but also inspires them. A lack of confidence shows greatly, like when you walk with your head down and when you avoid looking people in their eyes as you talk to them, when you speak softly and without authority, and when you're uncomfortably passive in a group of people. These traits of a lack of confidence give people a certain impression of who you are and whether they should listen to you or not. People buy into you before they buy into what you say. Without confidence, you've lost the battle before it even started.

If you're lacking in confidence, it usually means you're lacking in experience. Confidence comes from a series of successful attempts. If you want to condense time frames and become confident quicker, make sure you have a mentor. A mentor always excels your learning curve because they have grown through the area of life you are trying to grow in. Also, mentors are helpful because you have someone there to see what you're doing right and what you need to adjust, which is crucial. I remember a gentleman I coached on his confidence. He had been working by himself to build his confidence for months, but because he decided to get a mentor and have me guide him on how he could more confidently present himself, he was able to make great strides in just a couple of days. When you have a lack of confidence, not only are others beating you but you're also beating yourself. Don't let the first disease of insecurity consume you.

2. Caring What Others Think

Now I have seen this disease take out more people than I care to mention. The desire for others' approval is a devastating disease. This disease almost consumed me. Why do I say that? Because I am a recovering people-pleaser. I used to enjoy making people happy, sometimes at my own expense. I had to learn that I can't make everyone happy and I can't care what they think about me. When you care about what people think of you, you are a slave to their opinions. Their thoughts become anchors that are tied to your foot, sinking you to the bottom of the ocean. There is a quote by Goi Nasu that says, "An entire sea of water can't sink a ship unless it gets inside the ship." Similarly, the thoughts of the world can't put you down unless you allow them to get inside of you. I know you won't, because you are a crusader.

Most people care what other people think because they don't want to be talked about. I had to come to the realization that if I did badly, people would talk about me, and if I did well, people would talk about me, so why bother caring if they are going to talk about me anyway? If all of your happiness is wrapped up in the opinion of others, you will never be able to control when you are happy. The reason you care about what others think is because you want them to like you. Here is the truth: Everyone won't like you. In today's world, we have something called haters, and I don't even call them haters anymore. I call them "angry birds," like the old mobile game, because if you ever played the game *Angry Birds*, you know the whole objective is to knock down someone else's building, and that's what they want to do. They want to knock down your dreams, your hopes, and your aspirations, and you can't let them. Life is too short to be strung to others' opinions. You can't care what others think. Here is the three-step cure to dealing with this disease of insecurity.

Cure 1: Know Thyself

When you are clear about who you are and who you want to be, it is easy to put the cares and thoughts of others on the back burner. When you are living from a place of self-acceptance, you will realize that what people say or think about you has less to do with you and more to do with them. Most people only hate on that which they wish they could emulate. Take on the mindset that what people think of you is none of your business, because you are great and destined to do great things, and if you believe that, then what people say or do can't sway how you feel about yourself.

Cure 2: Remember How Far You Have Come

Most times, achievers or those who wish to be achievers are their own worst critics, which could be a blessing or a curse. If you don't take time to congratulate yourself, you will constantly portray to your subconscious mind that you are not good enough. How could you ever feel that you have achieved if you constantly move the needle of achievement? If your needle of achievement is 10 and you have been at 8 or 9 for a while, you start to say, "I know I can be a 13 or 15." When you achieve 11, you never celebrate the fact that you once wanted to be a 10 and surpassed that. Guess what? When you get to 11, you will be thinking you can be a 16 or 17. When you get to 14, you'll never celebrate because your mental needle will move again.

This is something that plagues most achievers, their desire to do more and be better than they were. If they took the time to look back, they would say, "Wow, I used to be an 8, and now I'm a 14!" I'm not saying to be content at 14, but be grateful you made it this far, and be excited for the opportunity to go farther.

Cure 3: Stop the Comparison

Your race has never been against others; it's always been against yourself. You're striving to become a better version of you this year than last year. For most successful people, the success of others motivates them to do more. The average person lets the success of others demotivate them from doing anything. What you have to understand is that other people's success is not your failure. Also, other people's lack of success should not be your failure either. With comparison, it can happen in two ways. One way is, you compare your lack of success to their success. You either say, because they are having all this success that means you can't have it, or you make yourself feel bad for their success, as if it makes you any less of a person.

The other way to compare yourself is to compare their lack of success to your lack of success, and you choose not to grow beyond yourself because you feel comfortable saying to yourself, "They aren't growing, so it's okay for me not to grow." The old adage is, water seeps to its own level. At times, if you watch when a new person joins an organization, look for the crowd he/she joins. If they join the high achievers, you know that's their true desire, and they don't mind hanging with the other high achievers and being stretched to do and be more. If they hang around the low achievers, you know they might have desires to be a high achiever but may not be willing to do the work to become one. Usually that has a lot to do with their belief in themselves.

Whether you compare yourself to high achievers or low achievers, just be careful not to base who you are and who you could be on those people's actions. If you do that, you have no control of your destiny. Your success would now be based on what others do and whether they do it well. Remember, you can look at high achievers and be motivated to do more, and look at lower achievers and know where you don't want to be. Also remember that you are running your race against yourself, and watching others should not dictate what you do or don't do.

3. Blame

Here it is, the last disease and the greatest disease of insecurity. If allowed, blame can be the biggest roadblock to you becoming one of the super successful. My biggest battle with blame started when I was in high school. My entire lack of success was always someone else's fault. When my grades weren't good, it was my teacher's fault because he wasn't a good enough teacher, or my father's fault because he wasn't in my life to help me. When I didn't make the varsity team, it was because the coach didn't like me. When my mom and I got into it, it was because she just didn't understand me. I never once looked at the fact that maybe I didn't study hard enough, or maybe I didn't wake up at 6:00 a.m. to practice my jump shot, or maybe my problems with my mom stemmed from me not doing the right things.

I didn't start realizing I was the problem until way into college, after I started to personally develop myself. The more I read positive books like the one you are reading now the more I started to realize the thinking patterns of the super successful. I remember the business I started when I was 18 and that first book I ever really read from cover to cover. It was given to me by a guy I started my business with, who is now one of my best friends, Mike Loubier. He gave me *Think and Grow Rich*. Even now, I don't know why he gave me that book first. That's a tough book to start your growth journey with, so if you're new to personal development, I wouldn't start with that book. However, that was the book that started me down the path of success.

As I read the book, I realized so many things about myself. The most significant thing I learned was that the biggest key to success was me. I had all the power in my own hands. I had spent my whole life trying to release my power out of other people's hands, not knowing it was in my hands the whole time. I thought it was the things that happened to me in my life that dictated my current circumstances. I thought it dictated me sleeping on my mom's couch, with no money in the bank, and working at Chuck E. Cheese's, a college dropout and a flat-out disgrace to myself. I realized it wasn't what happened to me; it was how I was responding to that adversity in my life. I love how Jim Rohn says, "The same wind blows on us all. The wind of disappointment, the wind of shame, the wind of doubt, but it's not the blowing of the wind that determines your destination; it's the set of the sail." I stayed in my situation of adversity so long because I kept trying to change the wind instead of setting the proper sail.

IT'S NOT THE BLOWING OF THE WIND THAT DETERMINES YOUR DESTINATION, IT'S THE SET OF THE SAIL

#TheMentalPlaybook
#MentalAsset

Sometimes we look at life and say, "The deck has been stacked against me," but TD Jakes says, "Someone can take the hand you have been dealt and win." I had to start doing the thing I had been avoiding for so long. I had to take responsibility. Some might ask, take responsibility for what? The answer is, for EVERY-THING!!! Wait, what do you mean everything? I mean everything. What if it's not my fault? Take responsibility! What if it was an accident? Take responsibility! What if I'm angry? Still take responsibility! Yes, I know it's hard, and I know our emotions get in the way. I know taking the high road gets tough, but it's the only way to take control of your life. When you blame, you give control to other people, because if it's someone else's fault, you can't move forward unless they fix it.

The power is in your hands and no one else's. Your life is the fruit of your doing or undoing. What the super successful do is take it a bit farther. Not only do they take responsibility for their doings, but they take more than their share of responsibility. The minute the CEO has someone in his organization who makes a mistake, it sends the company into free fall. If asked why the company is doing poorly, he blames the insubordinate employee, and the company will continue to go down. If a pastor blames the lack of church growth on the congregation or a nonprofit organization's founder blames the volunteers, then those establishments are going down. Regardless of the problems, a leader takes responsibility. Blame shows a high level of insecurity. Blame says, "I'm not strong enough to own my problems and fix them, so I'm going to put the problem on someone else." Taking responsibility is saying, "I know there is a problem, and I'm going to fix it." That's the separation from the average and the super achievers.

Chapter 10

Toxic Environment

*You are the average of the
five closest friends
you hang around with.*

I know all about toxic environments after growing up in some of the roughest neighborhoods in New York City. I watched toxic environments poison not only people but their children and grandchildren— generations tarnished by toxic environments driven by negative associations. I remember my grandmother saying that birds of a feather flock together, and at the time, I didn't really know what that meant, but now I realize she was speaking of association. She was trying to warn me that I needed to stay away from people who would bring me down. Most people don't realize the power of association.

Think about it though. If your friends drink, you probably drink too. If your friends speak with bad language, then you probably speak with bad language too. If your friends eat unhealthily, then you probably do too. On the contrary, if your friends exercise often, you probably do too. If your friends do volunteer work, you probably do too. Like attracts like! What surrounds us is usually within us, whether negative or positive. Your associations can create habits in your life. Habits dictate actions; actions dictate results; and results dictate lifestyle. Your lifestyle can be affected by the associates you choose to keep.

When I first got into business, someone told me I was the average of the five closest friends I hung around with. They said that if I added the income the five of us made per year and divided by five, I would get close to my yearly income. I didn't believe it, but I did the math and was shocked and angry all at the same time because it was true. Imagine if the five closest people to you started cursing every single day relentlessly. Even if you didn't want to curse, you would start hearing choice words come out your mouth over time. In the same breath, if they all started eating healthily, you would probably be compelled to eat healthily as well. Our associations can have a great impact on our decisions, and that's why it's so important to have the right people around you. Even a person with great potential can find themselves doing the wrong things because of negative associations. Potential can die in a toxic environment.

The tallest tree in the United States is in the Redwood Forest in California. Imagine if you took the same seed that grew into the tallest tree in America and instead of planting it in California, you planted it in Alaska. Would it still grow to be the tallest tree in America? The answer is obviously no, but why? The tree had the potential to be the tallest, but the environment is not conducive enough to allow the tree to grow to its potential. The dirt was not fertile enough; the sun wasn't present enough; and the water wasn't properly allocated. With those factors in place, potential was not enough, and I see a lot of people with a lot of potential but the environment they place themselves in sets them back. Like growing up in the wrong neighborhood, you might not be able to leave some environments right away, but even if you can't leave the environment physically, you must leave it mentally.

When I was in that same situation, I couldn't just leave at first, so I had to leave mentally. The friends I hung out with every day, I had to reduce that to one day a week. The ones I hung out with one day a week I had to hang out with for one hour a week, and some I had to disassociate from altogether. I didn't do that in a negative way. I just stopped being as available.

When my phone rang, I didn't answer as much, and when events came up, I was too busy to go. This was the way I stopped the toxic situations, the toxic conversations, and the toxic philosophies from getting into my cup of life. However, it's not enough to keep the toxic out of your cup. You must also flush out the old and toxic with clear, purified information. It's not enough to change your old associations. You must replace them with new ones.

Now when I first made my change, the best associations were not available to me, and even if they were, I don't think they would have let me in because I would have brought down their averages. I started to replace my old associations with the books of people who had success, and I listened to audios and went to seminars. I needed that purified information to get rid of the toxic information. I had to realize that 97 percent of people would not be super successful. If I wanted what the successful had, I had to do what they did and become what they became. The successful didn't become successful by associating with unsuccessful people. If you want to be a part of the elite, you must walk away from the 97 percent who don't desire the success you do. Those individuals are fine in their toxic waste, and they don't want to be bothered.

Here is one of the biggest mistakes I see from people leaving toxic environments. They try to bring people with them out of the toxic environment. First off, a sinking ship shouldn't SOS to another sinking ship. Some people, even if you throw them a life vest, would rather drown in their misery than be pulled into success. I decided that I had to sell out. I had to sell out, to leave, so I could come back and help out. This is why the flight attendant says to put your mask on first before assisting others. Once you get yourself out of the toxic environment and you become strong enough, then you can go back and help those who want to be helped out of the toxic waste. Just know that in order to separate yourself from the average, you must also separate yourself from the toxic.

A
SINKING
SHIP
SHOULDN'T
S.O.S.
TO
ANOTHER
SINKING
SHIP

#TheMentalPlaybook
#MentalAsset

– Chapter 11 –

Holding On

*Successful people learn to
hold on while others
have merely let go.*

There is a saying, "Successful people learn to hold on while others have merely let go." I agree with this statement when the successful hold on to their dream goals and ambitions. However, some people take that statement too far and hold on to the wrong people, past failures, current circumstances, hurts, and disappointments. Holding on could be the very thing that is pulling you down. We all must learn that, at times, we need to let go, whether it's letting go of those bad eating habits or letting go of your excuses for not going to the gym if you're trying to be healthy. At times, we need to learn to let go of the people who have become a burden in our lives. They are like anchors that weigh us down if we allow them to.

I remember one of my friends telling me a story about how he was going to Africa, and he had a few extra suitcases. The airport said he had to pay additional fees for the extra baggage he was carrying. I believe that's how life is; it charges us if we carry that extra baggage. We must learn to let go because holding on to the negativity won't serve you. Here's the biggest thing we need to learn to let go of, and that is our old philosophy. It's our mindset that we really need to strengthen in order to let things go. Because it's our personal philosophy that says we can't move forward from our failures, we decide to hold on to it. It is our mindset that says we need to hold on to our disappointment because we believe it will continue to happen to us anyway. It's our mentality that says we should hold on to a person even though we know being associated with them will take us farther and farther away from our goals. Here are four keys to letting go of the negatives you have been holding on to:

Be Thankful: Not only do you need to be thankful but you must also accept the truth. To let go, you must first be thankful for the experiences that made you laugh, that made you cry, and most importantly, that helped you learn and grow. Whatever you are letting go of, understand that everything happens for a reason, and whatever you went through was needed in order for you to walk into the destiny you were created for. Once you are thankful for those things and the lesson you learned, you must now accept the truth that the thing you were holding on to is no longer serving you and it's time to say goodbye.

Letting Go May Be Temporary: Understand that you might just need to let go for a while and not forever. You might only need to let go of some people and things for a while or until you get strong enough not to be influenced by them. Maybe you just need time to strengthen yourself so you're not swayed by outside forces. Now I must say this because some people will think I am saying to let go of their spouse, kids, or family, and I am not saying that. I am not promoting divorce or broken families! Rather, what I'm saying is that sometimes you have to mentally let go of the negativity that is around you.

I remember when I first started in business, and I had people who made fun of my venture, and I had to mentally let go of them even though they lived in my house. I had to stop having conversations with them about my dreams and goals. I was silly enough to come home and try to paint a vision for them about why I was so excited. I had to realize that if they had the vision I had, then they would be doing what I was doing.

If they saw what I saw, heard what I heard, and met who I met, maybe they would also get it, but because God didn't give them my vision, I can't get mad that they don't see it. I had to learn to let go emotionally and mentally. I had to go do what I needed to do in order to make my dreams a reality.

Take Responsibility: Sometimes people can't let go because they gave someone else or something else control. You can't let go of something that someone else is holding on to for you. You have to make the decision to take full responsibility for everything that has happened in your life. Get rid of the blame. You're not broke because your friends convinced you to go on vacation when you didn't have the money. You're not fat because you have kids or it's in your genes. You're not unhappy because of the guy or girl who left you. If you get this, your life will change forever! You are exactly where you are because of the choices you made. Until you fully accept this, you will be stuck in the life you don't want. When you choose to take responsibility, you take control. When it's someone or something else's fault, you can't change it, but when it's your fault, you can. You can be in control. The day you take control of your life is the day you will have the ability to be and do whatever you want to be and do. You can let go when you take control.

Focus Inward: Once you've taken responsibility, now focus all your energy on you and how you can be better and greater than you have ever been. I love Jim Rohn when he says, "Spend more time working on you than you do on your job." He also says, "If you have four hours to cut down a tree, you spend three hours sharpening the knife and one hour cutting the tree." Most people are whacking the tree of their life with a dull axe and wondering why they aren't seeing the tree fall. Your ability to let go is directly proportionate to your ability to grow. Pick up educational books, get a coach, go to seminars, listen to audios, and take classes. Do whatever you need to do to become better today than you were yesterday.

Most people walk into a New Year looking for new results, but they take the same person into the New Year. You can take this note to the grave: Staying the same person equals getting the same results. If you can focus on these things, you can learn to let go and stop holding on to the things that are killing your dreams. I want you to hold on to the aspirations, goals, and dreams for your life, but let go of the things that are not serving you. One last story on this point is that there was once a man at a door he could see through and see everything that God promised him, but for some reason, he couldn't get through the door. He prayed to God, saying, "God, why would you bring me so close to my goals even to the point where I can see them, but I can't get them?" And God responded, "Because there are people and things you're holding on to that I will not allow to step into the land of blessings, so when you let them go, I will let you go." We have to be like that man. If we let go of the things that don't serve us, we can start to achieve all the things we ever dreamed of.

WHEN
YOU
CHOOSE
TO TAKE
RESPONSIBILITY
THEN YOU
TAKE CONTROL

#TheMentalPlaybook
#MentalAsset

– Chapter 12 –

Emotional Instability

The mental and emotional
roller coaster.

If there were one phrase that could describe this chapter, it would be the mental and emotional roller coaster. During my journey, there have been times I have taken a ride on this roller coaster and even times I have been the conductor. The mental and emotional roller coaster is a series of situations that happen in your life, which you allowed to take you from hot to cold in an instant, or situations that take you from thinking clearly to thinking irrationally. This emotional instability can wreak havoc on your goal of becoming super successful. Here are signs that you're emotionally unstable, when you are faced with a problem and you shut down. Sometimes, depending on the problem, you shut down for the whole day. This is when you let one moment in your day dictate how you feel, react, and respond for the whole day. You hear these people saying, "I'm just having a horrible day." They don't realize that there is no such thing as a bad day, only a bad moment we allow to ruin our day because of our emotional instability.

Your level of frustration, anger, and annoyance explodes because of something that someone did to you or because of some bad thing that happened to you. Successful people know how to control their emotions so that when negative things arise, they respond instead of react. Reacting is making an immediate and illogical decision without thinking. Responding is taking time to think first and strategize on the best approach for the negativity they are currently facing. It's understanding how to think and respond to pressure. In life and success, pressure will always be there. More importantly, pressure is needed to give you the force necessary to move forward in life. When an archer shoots an arrow, in order to have it shot forward, he must first put pressure on the string and the arrow, bringing them backward with the pressure and force. That pressure and force are what propels the arrow forward in order to reach its target quickly.

It's when something happens to you that you don't like and the people around you leave because they know how you can become when you are disappointed. This becomes a problem when people can't trust you to be rational in the midst of problems, so they don't want to be around you at all based on your history in these situations. All successful people have a good team of people around them 24/7. You don't want that team on edge because they don't know what type of day you're having. Your team of people should never see you unable to handle situations. Their faith and belief is in you as their leader, and if you can't hold it together, how do you expect them to hold it together when problems arise? If they can't trust your strength to handle the situations that life brings your way, they will find someone else they can trust and believe in.

It's when something happens to you that you don't like and the people around you leave because they know how you can become when you are disappointed. This becomes a problem when people can't trust you to be rational in the midst of problems, so they don't want to be around you at all based on your history in these situations. This is crucial because all successful people have a good team of people around them 24/7. You don't want that team on edge because they don't know what type of day you're having. Your team of people should never see you unable to handle situations.

REACTING
IS
MAKING
AN
IMMEDIATE
AND
ILLOGICAL
DECISION
WITHOUT
THINKING

#TheMentalPlaybook
#MentalAsset

Their faith and belief is in you as their leader, and if you can't hold it together, how do you expect them to hold it together when problems arise? If they can't trust your strength to handle the situations that life brings your way, they will find someone else they can trust and believe in.

Last but not least, emotionally unstable people hurt people when they get hurt. It's like an instinct that says "an eye for an eye." You hurt me, and I will hurt you worse. This, to me, is the worst part of emotional instability because it shows a lack of maturity in that unstable person. Successful people walk away from tit-for-tat situations because it's not worth the time and it also gains nothing, because no one wins in the end. John C. Maxwell has a good line for this. He says, "Hurt people hurt people." What those hurt people must understand is that if someone's action hurts them and their response is always to hurt that person worse, then they are easily controlled by the actions of others. Successful people don't react to the provoking of others whether purposefully or not purposefully.

Why is this so important? If you thought you were going to succeed without going through hurts, then you have another think coming. If you're moving, you will get hurt. Someone will do or say something to you, or maybe they won't do something they promised you, but you have to take it and smile because allowing this to take you on an emotional roller coaster of negativity is not worth it, as you're putting your success in jeopardy by reacting. I love the movie *42*, which is a movie about the story of Jackie Robinson, the first African-American in Major League Baseball. There is a scene with Harrison Ford, who played the Major League Baseball executive who signed Jackie Robinson to play in the Major Leagues, named Branch Rickey. He was talking to him about the abuse he might take as a black man playing in Major League Baseball in the 1940s, a very turbulent time for blacks in America. Jackie Robinson, who was played by Chadwick Bosemen, said to Branch Rickey, "Do you want a player who doesn't have the guts to fight back?" Branch Rickey responded, "No, I want a player with the guts not to fight back." He went on to say, "People are not going to like this. They are going to do anything to get you to react. If you echo a curse with a curse, then they will hear only yours. If you follow a blow with a blow, they will say the Negro lost his temper and that you don't belong. Your enemy will be out in force, and you cannot meet him at his own low ground … Like our savior, you have to have the guts to turn the other cheek. Can you do it?" Jackie Robinson then responded with, "You give me a uniform, you give me a number on my back, and I will give you the guts."

I tell that story to illustrate the point that Jackie understood what Branch was saying. He was saying that if you go hurt for hurt, the ones who hurt you don't lose—you do. In order to get over the problem of emotional instability, you must understand the cycles of success. You can't have good without bad; you can't experience the joy of winning until you've felt the hurt of losing; and you can't have a rainbow without the rain or the testimony without the test. This cycle of success dictates that all emotions will be given to you on the journey, and you can't give in to them, but you must allow them to train you, learning to grow in every situation and working to find the lessons. When the mistakes are made or the situation arises again, you know how to handle it not just for yourself, but now you know how to take others through that cycle. It's important to learn how to find the good in every problem, the success in every failure, and the triumph in every tribulation. You can do that if you can respond by thinking about the best way for you to get the positive out of every negative situation. Then and only then can you beat emotional instability and take yourself off the emotional roller coaster, never to ride again.

– Chapter 13 –

The Unbalanced Life

*There is no such
thing as time management.*

What are the most important things in your life? If you polled the world, a large population would say God comes first, then family, then career. My question to you is, is that a factual statement, or is that a cute saying? The truth of the matter is that most people are more unbalanced than they care to admit. We make statements like "God first, family second, career third" because we are placing them as priorities in our lives. The truth of the matter is, most people say these are their priorities, but they don't show it. Here is the question you should ask yourself to determine what your true priorities are:

What do you spend your time doing? What you spend the most time doing would usually dictate what you value most. There are a few exceptions here but not many. I know in your mind you want to make your priorities be like that cute little saying, but if you look at reality, it's generally not that easy to practice. Now I'm not here to bash you on this because having a balanced life is impossible. I believe there is no such thing as having a balanced life; it's a lie. You will never have every aspect of your life equally balanced. What you should strive for is harmony. Sometimes there are things happening in your family life, like a wedding or funeral, where everything else gets pushed to the side because that's the priority. Sometimes there are things going on in your career, like a new promotion or the starting of a new business, that force you to spend more time at work than you do socially or with family. Sometimes you go on a week trip with the guys or gals, so you don't spend as much time with family or work. There are always going to be things to juggle, but the focus of making all these things line up to be exactly balanced all at the same time is ludicrous. If you know there will never be perfect balance, then you won't beat yourself up about being a bit unbalanced.

Having harmony can be done. In order to have harmony, you need to do two things. One is communicating with every person in every single area of your life and telling them what you are trying to do, how you are trying to do it, what you are going after, why you are going after it, and why it's important. You need to communicate with the coworkers and let them know why you can't go to happy hour after work because of the kids you need to spend time with or the goals you are going after. Let your family know this month is going to be hectic because of these things happening in your business. Let the family know what's happening so that when you are not around, there is no reason to be upset because you properly communicated to them about the unbalanced time. This makes your life unbalanced, but with the proper communication, you will have harmony. When you clearly communicate with the people in each area, it becomes easier to say no when asked if you can do something that goes against the harmony that you are working toward today. If you properly communicate, you can have good harmony.

When I hear people talk about work-life balance, I normally hear them talk about time management. There is no such thing as time management. If someone gave you time and asked you to manage it, what could you do? There are 24 hours in a day, and you can't change that. Time is constant. The only thing you can do is manage your schedule, which is the second thing you need for harmony. You need to open up your calendar and see how you are placing the things of importance in the most efficient way. I even put things like hanging out with my son on my calendar. It's not that I need a reminder to hang out with my son. It's that I am being strategic to say that this time in my schedule is dedicated, and no matter what happens in life, this time is dedicated to my son. This other time in my schedule is dedicated to hanging out with my wife. This other time in my schedule is dedicated to working on my business. This other time in my schedule is dedicated to working at my job. This other time in my schedule is dedicated to vacations. This other time in my schedule is dedicated to hanging out with my friends. You have to be that methodical with your schedule management in order to have the right harmony.

With all this said, I want to be clear that you do not have to neglect your commitments, give up your faith, or neglect your family to become successful. You do not have to drop everything you're doing to get to where you want to be in life. I think that's the biggest misconception about success—that you have to choose between one or the other. Excuse my language, but that is a bunch of bull. You don't have to sacrifice your spiritual obligation, your family, your health, or anything else to become successful.

In the same breath though, I am here to say that it does take some sacrifice in order to achieve success. Those who are super successful understand that sometimes you have to believe in a dichotomy, which means you have to believe in contradicting ideas at the same time. What do I mean by this? You might be saying that I just said you didn't have to sacrifice those things, but now I'm saying you have to make sacrifices. Okay, hear me out. Most people's brains go only black or white, and they don't know the art of balance when looking at their situations.

Here is what I mean. Yes, you should not sacrifice time with the family, but you can't spend all your time with the family because it won't get you to your goals. If you have spiritual obligations, you don't have to give them up, but you can't spend seven days a week at the church, do nothing toward your success, and expect to get there.

TIME IS
CONSTANT

#TheMentalPlaybook
#MentalAsset

It's all a balance between health, God, family, career, school, and everything else you deem a priority in your life. My wife has been trying to get me to take a salsa lesson, and balance is like a salsa dance. You have to move in a few different ways, but all of the movements add up to one dance. In a salsa dance, it's also a balance of the man's movement and the woman's movement, and if one is too dominant, then it doesn't look graceful, but it has to be a back-and-forth thing. This is how your life of harmony must be.

All of your priorities are movements, but they all add up to the same dance of happiness and success in your life. It's like parents who don't go on a vacation with their kids. It's not that they don't love the kids. It's that maybe on that vacation they needed some alone time to make the marriage work. It's all important. The kids are important, but so is the marriage. The church is important, but so is the family. The family is important, but so is the health. And the health is important, but so is the career. It's all important, and that's what most people miss about harmony.

As a young entrepreneur, I used to lean way too heavily on the sacrifice: give up your bowling night; stop being a DJ; and don't do that music you love. Instead, focus on the success first, and then all those other things will come. However, what I didn't realize was that when you do that, two things happen. You get burned out, and you don't have passion for what you're doing. If that happens, you end up never having the success you wanted in the first place. On the journey, it won't be a perfect harmony, but there can be harmony. Harmony is all about understanding that it's all important, but it all won't be balanced. If you are a woman, you might be a mom, a daughter, a wife, a minister, a singer, an investor, and a businesswoman all at the same time. All of these titles are important to you, and you want to achieve success in all of these arenas. If that is the case, you can't drop all to focus on one. You can't stop being a mom to make your career work, and you can't stop being a wife to make motherhood work. Now, although every title you hold is important, you have to make sure you do it strategically, like we talked about earlier.

Remind yourself of what is important, and make sure that when you strategize, you keep those things in mind. Make sure you properly define what success is to you. I don't want you to spend your time chasing an incorrect idea of success only to reach the end of your life and realize that you were chasing the wrong thing. Always remember that some sacrifices are not worth the reward. I have a son named Nathaniel, and if I have to completely drop being a dad in order to create success, I won't do it—some things are just not worth it. I grew up without a constant father figure, and I was grasping at straws to find someone who would father me. I would never want my son to have to deal with that. The good thing is that you don't have to. You can balance all that you have on your plate and still get to where you want to go.

Make sure to set goals for where you want to be in your life and in all of the areas of your life. Whether it's physical, emotional, spiritual, financial, or family, you must get your goals clearly defined. When you have adequate goals, you can come up with an adequate plan. One of my mentors told me that success is woven like tapestry, and you can't leave it up to chance. You must be clear about the outcome you want to achieve in your life. When you do this, it becomes easier to get a correctly aligned harmony you want to achieve.

– Chapter 14 –

Plow the Ground

Procrastination is the assassination
of your destination.

It's funny, ever since I decided I was going to be a high achiever, I constantly asked a question I'm sure you have asked many times as well. The question is, what is the secret to success? What is the one thing I can do that will get me to the elite levels of success? The truth is that there is no one secret of success, but if there were one, it would be this topic of plowing the ground. Plowing is an interesting concept. It's a farming process where either an animal or human will pull a machine across the ground, which does two things. It loosens the dirt by lifting the dirt up, and it makes lines in the ground.

The ground that has been plowed becomes a good place for farmers to grow crops. The problem with plowing is that it's hard work dragging that machine across acres and acres of land. With the hot sun in the springtime, it could make plowing a gruesome experience. Especially in the winter when it snows, the ground could become hard from freezing. Plowing an entire farmland is definitely not for the faint of heart. Well so is success. Its work is not for the faint of heart, which is why the majority of people never get the success they look for. There is a joke I used to use often, which was, if you ever wanted to hide anything, hide it in work and most will never find it. Most people run away from work. Sometimes hard work is like long, grueling hours in the sun, plowing frozen ground. It's tedious and tiring.

The thing I hate to hear the most is people who say these people are successful because they are lucky. No, it's not because they are lucky. It is because they worked their butts off. It's funny, the harder I work the luckier I get. Hard work is my best friend. Most people look for ways not to work hard. They look for the easy path. They look for a handout. Don't be like the average. Don't let laziness creep up on you like a malady. Your chance to create success lies in hard work. The fact is that success is usually disguised as hard work, so most people don't recognize it when it presents itself. Anyone who tells you that working hard is a waste of time is stupid. I hear people say the cliché "work smart not hard," but every high achiever I have ever met worked both hard and smart.

What stops you from working hard? For the everyday person who has work, kids, cooking, laundry, household errands, church, family, and the list can go on and on, how does that person do all those things and still work hard on their dreams? I know most people who are looking to be high achievers still have full-time responsibilities and are looking to become super successful part-time. I am here to tell you that it is possible. I have seen so many people do it in my lifetime, but the thing you must do is stop making excuses. Excuses are tools of the incompetent. They build monuments of nothingness, and those who excel in them seldom excel in anything else. Excuses don't explain, and explanations don't excuse.

Why am I being so hard on this? It's because we have to come to a point where we don't let little things cheat us out of our big opportunities. We have to be willing to do whatever it takes to win. Yes, you have work and have kids and do laundry and cook, but we all do, and the successful people find a way in spite of all the obstacles. The thing that strikes people down is their laziness. They spend the time they could be spending on their dreams by sleeping or catching up on TV, the internet, or social media. They say things like, "I had a long day. I'm tired," and, "I will do it tomorrow." The problem with that is, tomorrow becomes next week; next week becomes next month; next month becomes next year; and next year becomes never.

The funny thing is that most people believe working on their dream needs 150 hours a week of dedicated focus, but the truth of the matter is that if you spend between 10 and 20 hours a week on your goals, you will be on track to start achieving those goals on a part-time basis. Ten to 20 hours only adds up to 1.5 to 3 hours a day. That's not much at all. It just takes dedication and focus on what you really want. You do that, and as you start to achieve that part-time success, it will allow you to leverage yourself. Leveraging yourself will allow you to have the ability to go full-time on your dreams to become a high achiever.

Early on in my journey to high achievement, I heard these words, and they changed my life with one phrase. Jim Rohn said, "Work full-time on your job and part-time on your fortune." That statement helped me stop making excuses about all the things I wasn't doing and start plowing the ground. Everyone knows success takes work, but most people are lazy and they procrastinate. They never understand that procrastination is the assassination of their destination. Procrastination and laziness, I call these two things the silent assassins. If these things are dominating your life and stopping you from working hard and getting to the success you desire, there are four things you must do to destroy the silent assassins.

1) The first thing you must do is get organized. Most people get lazy and don't work on their dreams because they have not organized what they want, why they want it, and what they are going to do to get it. They haven't organized what they want this year, this quarter, this month, this week, and today. They haven't organized a daily method of operation to be effective with the time they have, so that they don't waste time doing things that don't matter.

2) Understand that procrastination is a habit. If you have a lack of discipline in one area of your life, it will spill into other areas too. It will become a habit that needs to be addressed.

PROCRASTINATION IS THE ASSASSINATION OF YOUR DESTINATION

#TheMentalPlaybook
#MentalAsset

Habits can't be eradicated; they can only be replaced. You must replace it with doing what you say you are going to do as soon as you say it. When you do it, reward yourself, no matter how small, because if you do this, you create a positive anchor in your subconscious that says, "I get good things when I act immediately."

3) Laziness is a state of mind, and the best way to change a mental state is to break the patterns of thought. Think about it. When you feel lazy, what feeling do you get? Do you feel tired? Do you have a lack of energy? Unmotivated? Uninspired? The main questions are, what gives you energy? What gets you excited? What motivates you? When you are feeling excited or motivated, do you listen to those emotions and put yourself into an excited state? When you change the questions you ask yourself, it will get you to focus on the things that can change your state. When you change your state when you are feeling lazy, you will change your attitude about how you are really feeling and break your laziness. You realize you might not be feeling lazy; you might just be a little tired. Switching your language from being lazy to being a little tired will

change the state you are in. That change of state will allow you to make different decisions. In a state of laziness, you might say, "Since I feel lazy, I'm shutting it down for the day." If you say, "I'm feeling a little tired," that state may make you decide you need to take a little nap and will get back at it in an hour. Just changing the questions you ask yourself can change the words you use to describe the situation. That change in language can change your state, which can change your outcome.

4) Think about all the things you gain when you actually do what you're supposed to do and do not procrastinate. Think about the person you will become by doing what you said you would do. Think about the things you will get, the people you will help, and the fun you will have if you just follow through and don't push it off to tomorrow. Focus on the promise of the future and not the pain of the present. If you're constantly reminding yourself of why you're doing what you're doing, it will encourage you to keep doing it.

FOCUS ON THE PROMISE OF THE FUTURE AND NOT THE PAIN OF THE PRESENT

#TheMentalPlaybook
#MentalAsset

– Chapter 15 –

The Failure Perspective

*The fear of failure has been
programmed into us
since we were kids.*

Looking back to when I was 18 and first starting in the world of business, I was so green that I didn't know how to deal with the word *failure*. In today's society, failure is a really bad word. When we were kids, we never wanted to fail a test or a class. When you play sports, you never want to fail to win or to score. When you're working a job, you never want to fail to complete a project or fail to it do it correctly. When becoming a parent, the biggest fear is to be a failure as a parent. When people get married, they don't want to feel like they are failing to be a good husband or wife. As you get older, you don't want to be a failure at setting yourself up for retirement. As it all comes to the end of your life, you don't want to look back, on your deathbed, saying, "I failed to fulfill my purpose."

This fear of failure has been programmed into us since we were kids and continues all throughout our adult life. Most people allow fear to cripple them, and because they're so afraid to fail, they never try. As a leader in this generation, I want to be the one who hammers down the philosophy that failure is not a bad thing. It's not this evil thing that you must avoid at all costs. The problem is the way we define it. Most people don't know the difference between being a failure and failing. Being a failure is the state of feeling and deciding to stay there forever. Failing is the state of doing something wrong or incorrect and learning from that mistake, picking yourself up, and continuing to move forward. One of my favorite quotes in the Bible is "though a righteous man falls seven times, he rises again." (Proverbs 24:16) When you make a mistake and fail, if you learn to allow it to be a teachable moment, it can never be failure.

John C. Maxwell has a book called *Failing Forward*. That's what you have to do, fail but continue to move forward. I love this quote by Michael Jordan: "I've missed more than 9,000 shots in my career. I've lost almost 300 games. Twenty-six times I've been trusted to take the game-winning shot and missed. I've failed over and over and over again in my life, and that is why I succeed." Failure actually propels you to success. When you fail, you learn what doesn't work and what to stay away from. Jim Rohn said, "You learn more by losing than you do by winning."

Here's the problem with the word *failure*. Most people haven't learned how to put failure into proper perspective. We can complain that the rose bushes have thorns or rejoice because thorn bushes have roses. When you change the way you look at things, the way you look at things will change. It seems crazy to me that we all know perfect is impossible, yet we try to avoid failing, in essence looking for a way to be perfect. The super achievers have learned to change their perspective on failure. They know failure is a possibility, and they know that even if they fail, they will learn valuable lessons in that failure, which will make them better at the next attempt. Actually, a "failed" attempt becomes a learning success.

Have you ever heard the saying "failure is inevitable"? Well I don't believe that. Okay, I believe that's partially correct; I believe failure can be avoided if you don't try. You can avoid failing by never getting in the game. If you don't get in the game, then you fail to achieve by default. The fear of failure tries to cripple those who are looking to be super achievers. Fear tries to kill their future growth by making them worry about something that may or may not even happen. If you attempt something, you may achieve it or you may fail, but you never know if you don't try. The thought of coming up short normally stops those from taking action. The worry overtakes them. Ninety percent of the things you worry about never come to pass. Some of us are worrying about failure, and failure might not ever come, and if it does and we put the proper perspective on it, we don't get disappointed because we realize that it's a part of the process of success. What happens if I know it's a part of the process, but I want to know some simple steps to overcoming that failure when it arises in my life? Here are five steps to put in place to overcome your feeling of failure:

1) Forget about how others will view you if you fail. Look, successful people know that people are going to talk about them when they fail and people are going to talk about them when they succeed. What I try to remember is that I'm not as good as they say I am. Saying this, I keep my ego in check. And I'm not as bad as they say I am. Saying this, I keeping my insecurity in check. One thing you can count on is that most people only care about your failures because they are too cow-ardly to go after what they really want due to their fear of failure. If they were going after all their goals and dreams, they wouldn't have time to notice your failures. Most people hate on others only because they have no clue of the effort and the blood, sweat, and tears that go into going after your goals.

2) Expect to make mistakes. We talked about this earlier, but just know that mistakes will show up, and if you have the proper perspective, you will learn from the failure, not get mad at it.

3) Remind yourself that you are good enough. Most people fear failure because they feel they don't have what it takes to succeed, but if no one has ever told you, then I am going to tell you right here and right now that you have greatness inside of you. You can be and do anything you set your mind to. Remember that the fear is not real.

I'M NOT
AS GOOD
AS THEY SAY I AM,
SAYING THIS, I KEEP
MY EGO IN CHECK.
AND
I'M NOT AS BAD
AS THEY SAY I AM.
SAYING THIS I KEEP
MY INSECURITY
IN CHECK

#TheMentalPlaybook
#MentalAsset

It is a product of thoughts that we create in our own mind, and we have the power to choose to accept them or deny them. You can always overcome failure, and just because you failed doesn't mean you can't do it. It just means you didn't do it this time. Thomas Edison was said to have failed 1,000 times trying to create the light bulb. His perspective wasn't that he didn't fail. It was that he found 1,000 ways not to make a light bulb. On the 1,001st attempt, he was able to figure it out, but what if he would've quit prior to the breakthrough? All of his failures played a part in helping him figure out the successful way to do it. He kept the faith in himself and trusted that he could do it. Don't lose faith in yourself, even if you don't get it the first time.

4) Review what your failure has taught you. Going back to the Thomas Edison story, he studied those failures, and after studying the failures, he crafted what would become his success. When you fail to do something, grab a notebook and a pen, and start to take notes on what went well, what went wrong, and what changes you will make in the future to turn that failure into a success. Experience teaches better than a book.

Taking notes on your experiences will become the blueprint to future success.

5) Get up and try again! There was a song in 2009 called "Try Again," written by Aaliyah. The main line in the song was, "If at first you don't succeed, dust yourself off and try again." Those lyrics encapsulate what it means to overcome failure. Know when and how to pick yourself up. Your strength is not measured when you're at your strongest but when you are at your weakest. It takes strength to get up when you have fallen, but those who have learned to create massive success have learned to master the art of bouncing back after they have fallen. Whether it's athletes losing big games, comedians having a horrible set, or actors not getting the part in the movie, they bounce back after failure and come back even stronger the next time. Learning how to deal with failure will definitely teach you how to be a super achiever.

– Chapter 16 –

The Directionless

The problem with the directionless
is not that they don't have a path;
it's that they don't even
believe in having a path.

Ups, downs, side to side. North, south, east, west, right, left, around and around. This is the path of the directionless, having no idea where they're going. They haven't taken the time to figure it out. The problem with the directionless is not that they don't have a path; it's that they don't even believe in having a path. They have sayings like, "It will all work out. I just have to sit here and do nothing and wait," or, "If I just wait, all the success I have ever wanted will land in my lap." Please don't be one of these people. Don't be directionless! The directionless have no plans, no goals, and no focus. The directionless are usually the ones who sit on the couch, eating chips and watching TV or playing video games all day.

A lot of times, the directionless struggle with finding enough motivation to do anything worthwhile. The reason for this is, they forget that motivation is an inward-outward thing, not an outward-inward thing. Most directionless people are waiting for someone to come and motivate them instead of creating that motivation within themselves. They want someone to create an environment that would stimulate their motivation. What they must do is find ways to motivate themselves. They can also figure out what demotivates them. Are you having trouble getting motivated to achieve? Are you becoming one of the directionless? If so, here are the top five things that kill the average person's motivation.

Killers of Motivation

Poor health is a huge reason people are unmotivated and become directionless. Newton's law states that a body at rest tends to stay at rest, and a body in motion tends to stay in motion. Usually lack of physical health is due to lack of motion. Getting up and getting your body out of rest mode and into action is important for proper health and is key to living a life of achievement. Some people overthink the proper health thing. You don't need 20 different diets, and you don't need to spend tens of thousands of dollars on a personal trainer. It's simple: eat right and exercise! You know what that means.

THE DIRECTIONLESS HAVE NO PLANS, NO GOALS, AND NO FOCUS

#TheMentalPlaybook
#MentalAsset

Put down the burger and have a salad sometimes, run around the block, and just be active! A body in poor health doesn't have the energy to go out and achieve everything it is destined to. Along with eating healthy and exercising, be sure to get a good amount of rest.

Inaction is another killer of motivation. Back to Newton's theory, it states that a body at rest tends to stay at rest. That part is poor health. The next part of that theory is, a body in motion tends to stay in motion. That part is about taking action! Once you start moving, it's easy to get inspired to keep moving because you see progress. Most people are looking for quantum leaps of success when the truth is that success happens moment by moment, one day at a time. As you see progress happening, your motivation continues to rise.

Human nature desires to see progress continue, and your continued action kills your inaction instantly. Sometimes you have to lower your bar in order to kill inaction. If you keep focusing on making it to a goal that's so far away, it becomes unbelievable and you won't take action. When I coach my employees on this, I tell them to find out what their ultimate goal is five years from now. They tell me, and I say, "What can you accomplish in this year that will get you closer to that ultimate goal?" If you do the process that way and focus on the day-to-day things instead of focusing on the ultimate goal, you will cure the inaction and start to head toward the goal step by step. The journey of 1,000 miles begins with the first step. Success doesn't happen in a day; it happens daily. And most people overestimate what they can do in a few months and underestimate what they can do when taking the necessary daily steps over the course of a year.

Overwhelm is an interesting killer of motivation. There is no motivation to do anything when you're trying to do everything. You can be sitting around for hours, thinking about all the things you have to do, and just that action gives you a feeling of being overwhelmed. I have found myself wasting precious time doing that. Overwhelm comes from putting too many projects on the plate and then trying to eat all the projects on the plate at the same time. Something you can do to help with the overwhelm is to subtract some of the unimportant projects and delegate them to someone else. Another is to organize the projects. You have to find out which ones will excite you the most and list them in levels of what will excite you. Whatever is the most important to you, schedule times to do these tasks. Once you have it broken down into bite-sized pieces, figure out when you choose to eat each piece. Schedule a time for a break or vacation every 90 days to prevent burnout. Sometimes the major stress of overwhelm comes from running for so long without a break.

Impatience can suck out your motivation. After getting your body in order, taking action, and handling overwhelm, sometimes you have to wait for the magic to happen. We live in an instant-gratification society. I want it now, hurry up, and let's go! Fast food is too slow, and 30-minute deliveries are not fast enough. Waiting for the success to show can be a demotivator but only if you're looking at it based on the ultimate goal. If you praise yourself for the little wins all along the way to the ultimate goal, you can remove some of that impatience. Impatience is the insidious thing that creeps up when we are in a hurry. Impatience is the thing that makes us fumble the ball because we already moved on to the next step. It's what causes us to put in half of the work and expect full pay. Impatience is never in the present because it's rushing into the future. When you start to get impatient, go back to your ultimate goal plan that is broken down from five years to every day. When you look at that, most times you will realize you're further ahead than you planned, and if you're not, you can put objectives in place to get you to the next step. Also, with impatience, you just have to have faith in the success process. Success is a journey not a destination. It takes time to grow and to mature. You wouldn't plant a seed today and go outside looking for a harvest tomorrow—that would be insane. Your success works in the same way. You plant your seed, give it constant water and sunlight, and in time, you will receive the harvest.

Loss of purpose would demotivate anyone. A lot of times, we try to motivate ourselves with things we want. You might go back to your ultimate goal and still feel unmotivated. That could be because your ultimate goal has one person who gains when it is achieved. That person is YOU! Goals that are self-driven work for a while, but long-term they always burn out and lose their effectiveness. This is because human beings at their core know they were created to do something greater than just gain for themselves. We desire to make an impact on things bigger than ourselves. Not saying those things for yourself are bad, but understand that you must find a purpose that is bigger than yourself if you want that lifelong motivation.

Have you ever seen someone doing the same thing for 50 years and wondered how that person cannot be bored? That's because that person found something that not only blesses them and makes them happy, but it also blesses those around them, which gives them a larger sense of meaning, and that meaning gives them motivation. Align your ultimate goal with your ultimate purpose, and you will become a man or woman who cannot be stopped. You will never want for motivation; you will wake the sun up with your passion. You will drive others to greatness.

IMPATIENCE IS THE THING THAT MAKES US FUMBLE THE BALL BECAUSE WE ALREADY MOVED ONTO THE NEXT STEP

#TheMentalPlaybook
#MentalAsset

You will become motivation to the name. You will not only have direction for yourself, but your clarity will give others direction and the key to developing out of being directionless. Finding the proper motivation that will give you direction means finding an ultimate goal and aligning it with your ultimate purpose, taking action, and having faith in the process.

ALIGN YOUR ULTIMATE GOAL WITH YOUR ULTIMATE PUR-POSE
AND YOU WILL BECOME A MAN OR WOMAN THAT CANNOT BE STOPPED

#TheMentalPlaybook
#MentalAsset

– Chapter 17 –

The Inner Loser

You have two sets of thoughts:
one is pulling you closer to
what you want; the other is not.

Have you ever talked to yourself? I bet something in your mind is saying, "I don't talk to myself!" That's it—that statement is you talking to yourself. I say that jokingly, but seriously too. Have you ever had voices in your head telling you to do or not do something? Those thoughts you have sometimes conflict with each other. They can be your best allies or your worst enemies. I had to learn to understand that thoughts are things, and those thoughts create your philosophies, and your philosophies dictate your actions, and consistent actions dictate your habits, and your habits create your lifestyle, but it all starts with thoughts. How do you respond to the thoughts that will bring you closer to your goals, not farther away?

You have two sets of thoughts. One set of thoughts is pulling you closer to what you want, helping you through the tough times, and getting you past adversity. The other set of thoughts is telling you that your dream can't be realized, that there is no hope, and that you shouldn't even try. That, my friend, is what I call the inner loser. When it comes to success, it's really a battle between the inner winner and the inner loser. The truth of the matter is that everyone has an inner loser inside of them speaking doubt and discouragement. Even the super successful have the inner loser inside of them. The super successful have learned to do one thing in order not to be overcome by the inner loser.

To explain how they do it, I want to tell a quick story. There was once a tribal leader teaching his grandson about life. The grandfather said, "Son, there is a fight constantly going on inside of you. It's a terrible fight between two dogs. One dog is evil, angry, envious, sorrowful, regretful, greedy, arrogant, and mean. The other is good. He is joy, peace, love, hope, humility, benevolence, generosity, truth, and compassion. The same fight that is going on inside of you is also going on inside me and everyone else in the world." The grandson thought about it for a minute and then asked his grandfather, "Well if this fight is going on, which dog will win?" His grandfather responded, "The one you feed the most." This is the exact situation happening to you right now. The inner winner and the inner loser are in constant battle, and the super successful win because they don't feed the inner loser.

They ignore it. When the inner loser speaks, they put their Beats headphones on. There is a great commercial about the Beats headphones by Apple, where great sports athletes are walking into the stadium, past hundreds of fans who are yelling and cursing them, but they have their headphones on, and all they hear is the music. They are zoning out the critics. This is what you have to do in real life. You have to put your Beats headphones on and only allow the inner winner to speak. When you learn to do this, you will have what I like to call the mental advantage. Those who know how to take control over their mind, their emotions, and their thought patterns have the advantage over every person who doesn't. If you change your mind, you change the game! You have all the power to dominate the game of life and get out of it everything you were destined to get. You must learn how to silence the inner loser and increase the volume of the inner winner.

How Do You Silence the Inner Loser?

If the negative thoughts pop up in your mind, telling you that you're not good enough, that you can't make it, that it's too hard, or that you can't do it, then you must make a conscious choice to remind yourself what the inner winner says. The inner winner we have in all of us says that you can do it, that you're the best, that success is yours, and to keep on going. Even if you don't fully believe the inner winner and you think the inner winner is full of it, do what the inner winner says and you are on your way to success. What if you're not sure what the inner winner and loser sound like? Let me give you some examples. The inner loser says to the athlete, it's too early to get up, work out, run, and do drills. The inner winner is saying, if you work while everyone is sleeping, then you will get to a point where you are the greatest athlete in the world, while everyone else is dreaming about it. The inner loser is saying to the businessman, don't worry about going to your meeting today; it's been a long day, so just relax. The inner winner is saying, this next meeting could be the difference between an okay business or an explosion in your business. The inner loser is telling the salesman, you have made enough calls; let's call it a day. The inner winner says, come on, you can do 10 more calls. The inner winner and loser are easy to tell apart because the inner loser is usually the one discouraging you, and the inner winner is usually encouraging you. Take the encouragement, listen to it, and run with it.

There is one thing I didn't get to talk about, and that's listening to other people's inner loser. Napoleon Hill says the number-one thing that holds people back from success is listening to their friends, family, and neighbors. These are the hardest people to hear it from because you love them and you know they want the best for you. They just don't realize when they say hurtful things or make jokes about you going for your goals and dreams that they are spewing their inner loser into your mind. Usually when someone tells you that you can't do something, it's because they don't believe they can do it, so they try to push their lack of belief onto you. Look, if you bought a brand-new $5 million house, and you had a special, white, imported carpet from Germany, and your friend came over with a bag of wet, nasty trash and started pouring it out all out over your white, imported carpet, how would you feel? Most people would be extremely upset. Well if you feel that way about a carpet, why do you allow people to pour out their wet, nasty, trashy thoughts in your mind?

Yes, I know this is a paradigm shift for most people. Most people don't perceive other people trying to push their inner loser onto them. I remember early on in my business career, I had friends and family who made jokes about my choice to chase my dreams, and I had to decide that I would not let anyone's inner loser affect my inner winner. In that situation, I had to remove those whose thoughts didn't align with my inner winner. There are people out there who choose to listen to their inner winner. Find those people and align yourself with them. The more you surround yourself with people who listen to their inner winner the more you will listen to your inner winner, and the more you listen to your inner winner the more you drown out the voice of the inner loser, until you can't even hear the inner loser at all. The more you do this the more you start to gain the mental advantage. This advantage is probably the most important ingredient to living the lifestyle of your dreams and not just watching and admiring the super successful but becoming one of the super successful.

THE MORE
YOU
SURROUND YOURSELF
WITH PEOPLE WHO
LISTEN
TO THEIR
INNER WINNER,
THE MORE YOU WILL
LISTEN TO YOUR
INNER WINNER
#TheMentalPlaybook
#MentalAsset

Final Thoughts

Before I give a closing statement, I want to thank you for your time and attention. There are a million things that you can spend your time doing, and you decided to take your time, energy, and resources to read this book, and for that, I am grateful. It was very important to me that I create a book that I believed would allow you to turn your mind into an asset instead of a liability. I took all the concepts I thought were important to mindset mastery and put them in as simple of terms as possible. I restated points to lock in the message, and I gave you practical tips so that you can always come back to this book. I hope this book can become a resource for you so that when you are trying to remember how to create a habit, how to turn fear into faith, or how to shift your perspective, you can come back to the chapters in this book and get a reminder to use it to push your life forward.

When I think about the high achiever and the people who have created the most success in their life, I know that these principles can put you right up there with some of the greats. There is not a person on the planet who has created a high level of success without learning to master the mind, whether directly or indirectly. You now have the blueprint. You now have the playbook to study, to win the championship of life. With everything in this book, I hope that you got every practical and philosophical tip that you can use to help you in your life, your business, your relationships, and all areas of your life. I am excited for your journey to success, and if I can ever be of assistance to you in any way, feel free to inbox me on social media. I wish you all success and fulfillment.

I believe in your ability to succeed.

I believe in your ability to master you mind.

I believe you can succeed on demand.

And I believe you can achieve at the highest level possible.

Good luck my friends! *Eugene Johnson*

WHAT TO DO WITH THIS INFORMATION: THE NEXT STEP

If you are like me than you love books but the truth is that most people never finish the books that they start. So, first I want to say congratulations for getting through this entire book and being committed to mental mastery. This mental matrix is a game changer for anyone who decides to put this information into practice.

Anyone who knows about mastering any topic knows that the only way to truly master anything is continuous learning. So, if you are committed to learning more on mastering the mental matrix I have created a comprehensive course on mindset mastery called Make Your

Mind an Asset online course. This course is dedicated to walk with you on the journey to mastery. Inside I ask the hard questions and help you form strategies you can implement in your finances, your business and in your life. This course was built for groups, corporate executive, sales leaders and entrepreneurs. Together we will break down all mental limitations and habits that are not serving you. Your mind is an asset, let's make sure you get it to consistently operate like it.

www.MakeYourMindanAsset.com

ABOUT THE AUTHOR

As a lifetime entrepreneur, Eugene has sold and marketed everything from consumer products, cloud technology to legal services. Eugene is currently the CEO and founder of Zyrl a social media marketing company with the mission of building the most dominant and revolutionary force in online marketing technology. Eugene is also an investor and an internationally known speaker and trainer.

Eugene has trained tens of thousands of people online with his videos gaining millions of minutes watched, hundreds of thousands of fans and million views is just under a year. There are CEO's, business leaders, entrepreneurs and sales executives all over the country that have all referred to Eugene as "The future of the personal development industry." With almost a decade and a half of experience in marketing, sales, coaching, business, public speaking, and leadership, he leads the pack directing and guiding people to success.

Starting from humble beginnings, he grew up in one of the worst neighborhoods in New York City and often found himself caught up in the troubles of living

in an impoverished area. Though his circumstances were not ideal, he had dreams of
taking his life to unprecedented heights. Eugene's high energy and exciting style, as well as his down to earth and easy to understand approach has touched the hearts of the many he has reached.

Eugene is that positive voice in your ear telling you to have faith, work hard, believe in yourself, and never quit. Eugene's favorite slogan is "Let no man steal your vision, because no man gave it to you."

Social handles:
Instagram – @EugeneKJohnson
Facebook – @EugeneKJohnsonOfficial–
Twitter – @EugeneKJohnson
LinkedIn – https://www.linkedin.com/in/eugenejohnson208
Snapchat – below

Email:
Eugene@Zyrl.us

Website:
www.EugeneJohnson.com

FOR TEAMS & ORGANIZATIONS

BRING THE TRANFORMTIONAL CONCEPT OF THE MENTAL MATRIX TO YOUR
ORGANIZATION

 Bulk pricing available: Support@eugenejohnson.com

51493977R00193

Made in the USA
San Bernardino, CA
24 July 2017